AF538861

AMITAV GHOSH
A CRITICAL STUDY

Shubha Tiwari

ATLANTIC
PUBLISHERS & DISTRIBUTORS (P) LTD

Published by

ATLANTIC

PUBLISHERS & DISTRIBUTORS (P) LTD

7/22, Ansari Road, Darya Ganj, New Delhi-110002
Phones : +91-11-40775252, 23273880, 23275880, 23280451
Fax : +91-11-23285873
Web : www.atlanticbooks.com
E-mail : orders@atlanticbooks.com

Branch Office
5, Nallathambi Street, Wallajah Road, Chennai-600002
Phones : +91-44-64611085, 32413319
E-mail : chennai@atlanticbooks.com

Reprint 2008, 2015, 2019

Printed in India at Nice Printing Press, A-33/3A, Site-IV, Industrial Area, Sahibabad, Ghaziabad, U.P.

Preface

Literature and its analysis perform many tasks. It preserves human consciousness. It refines sensibilities. It provides entertainment and relaxation. It reflects ethos of a people and a period of time. This can be an endless list. But the remarkable rise of Indian Writing in English reflects, above everything else, the desire of the reader to find herself/himself in a text. Literature and its analysis should have a bearing, howsoever, remote to the immediate conditions of the reader. Till two decades back we were happily reading alien stuff. We are still doing so. But our own existence has dramatically magnified for us. The maid servant, the pan shopkeeper, the middle glass teacher and the whole brand of typical Indian characters have filled pages. Life in relation to India has been sung in all details. This is absolutely fabulous.

Related to this development is the thought of decolonization and a diminutive term used for it by some critics, nativism (*desivad*). As a reader, I have to clarify my position on it. Everyone has to do it for oneself. Let us take the example of Amitav Ghosh. For Ghosh colonisation and related processes work is a permanent referent. He just cannot move out of this paradigm. Whatever he may write, this perspective is always there somewhere in his mind as a guiding principle. Yet, he does not take fixed positions. Grandiose depiction of our heritage and intellectual inbreeding in the name of decolonisation cannot be accepted. At the same time Western greed, inherent desire for domination, and exploitation need to be exposed. It is a tight rope walk. We cannot afford to tilt to either side. Ghosh talks of double standards of the West and still the unhygienic conditions in India, corruption as life style and other evils do not go unnoticed by him. An intellectual should not pawn her/his freedom to think at any cost. Whatever the temptations, free and rational research and thinking must go on. We are living among dangerous trends. Every uttering is construed as a sociopolitical statement. Harvesting profits by tilting to sides may be good business; it is bad academics.

A critic's job is to extend a tale, carry out its implications, gauge its effects, predict its future, establish its parallels and so on. In this role a critic is a creator. To write a sentence with ten references in it may be a great achievement but for me understanding, explaining and demystifying the text remain to be the prime tasks of a critic. Working as a bridge between the author and the reader, the critic can hardly afford to be lost in intellectual jigsaw. These are my purely personal views. Establishing the relation between life and literature is essential. Whatever the critic writes must have a bearing to the way she/he looks at the world, perceives literature or in short what she/he actually is. Weaving words, in a separate compartment, severed from personal thought seems futile to me. As hinted above, the intellectual must not go into patenting ideas for personal gains or for any other purpose. X takes Australian literature, Y captures Indian Poetics, and Z's domain is feminism. To me, this is absurd. One must exercise one's freedom to pick and choose one's ideas, to change and remodel them. Where is the need to cling to an idea for life? As round characters, we have to grow. We can change our ideas. We can contradict ourselves, if necessary. We can modify our thinking; we should, rather.

Amitav Ghosh has been an excellent choice for me to connect to my realities. He has been a superb medium for me to express my ideas. He has clarified my world to some extent. Whether it is the Western sense of superiority, Indian politics, pollution, international borders, the relation between childhood and adulthood, scientific research, art, music, culture, nuclear lobbies, world wars, communal hatred or riots, Ghosh has been my storehouse of ideas. He is suggestive. He is a thinking reader's author. His novels expand over vast areas of subjects. This is what makes him suitable for discussion. And the class of this author is evident by itself. His treatment of subjects is ever so sensitive.

A word may be said about language. We, those who live in the world of words, know that the status of language has changed over the years. Writing as a ceremony is totally out. Only some decades back anyone who held a pen and sat down to write took her/his work to be in the category of *craft*. It is no longer so. It is better this way. Language is employed in the coming pages only with a utilitarian aim—no *craft*, no *art*. Language is a tool of communication. It should be used only to get conveyed.

I am thankful to Dr. K.R. Gupta, Chairman, Atlantic Publishers and Distributors, New Delhi for snowing faith in me by bringing out this book. With his ever expanding and prospering publishing house, he has done, a lot in bringing quality to published critical material regarding literatures in English.

SHUBHA TIWARI

CONTENTS

1
Introduction

A writer gives herself/himself to the world. A secretive person cannot be a writer. The innermost processes of an individual's psyche fill the pages and then only the writing becomes valuable. What is the appeal of a piece of writing? The attraction comes exactly in proportion as to how much the author has unravelled herself/himself. To what extent the author has been successful in sharing her/his self with the reader—this decides the charm of a work. To be able to laugh and cry in your pages is the criterion of ability for a writer. The story line, the plot, the movement and the structure—all these are peripheral. The core lies with the giving away of herself/himself on the writer's part. A writer must not hold back. As we all know, the purging effect of literature is crucial. We read books to free ourselves of our pain and tensions and also to relive our joys. This is possible only when we have a candid work before us. As Whitman says of his book, 'When you touch my book, you touch my heart.' Craft may be important—yes, it is important. But sincerity is supreme. I cannot enjoy with a writer who holds herself/himself back. I just want my writer to let loose herself/himself. Probably, this is the reason many famous writers become unreadable for me. Pundits of criticism forbid the use of 'I, me, myself' in criticism. But I say that everything in this world is personal; if it is not personal, it is not real. The solidity and validity comes only when things get personal. Detached talk may be good philosophy but it cannot be good literature. And the genuineness shows, no matter what. The writer's personality spills over the pages. Objective observation, impartial judgement, detached analysis—all these are fanciful phrases with which a writer tries to positively influence her/his readers. But at the end of the day, the innermost self and experiences count. This is why when Naipaul talks about indentured labours, the world listens. Destovisky talks of death and dictatorship, you have to listens. Gunter Grass talks of Nazi oppression and he cannot be put aside. Gao Xingjian tells of Tiananmen massacre and you pay heed. It is like that. Individual is everything. Individuals are institutions, individuals are governments, individuals are departments. And above everything else, individuals are books and books are individuals. Books breathe and live. The writer lives there. Her/his most private moments are there. The heart of a writer is there for everybody's inspection—open to rebuke, appreciation and analysis. It is with this attitude I touch a book. No specific technique of criticism has been followed in the coming pages. The concerns such as why a character acts the way she/he does or how the author must have reached a particular conclusion, fill the pages. It is a sort of an explanation of the texts; an extension of the ongoing tale. My own thoughts often muddle up things. It is the joy of saying things I wanted to say. This can hardly be called criticism. At best, it can be called 'comments.'

Amitav Ghosh is talented. He is innovative. He is an experimentalist. He experiments extensively with the form of his books. But basically ideas run his books. Ideas are the driving force of his books. Each book of Ghosh is born out of a conviction. This is great. He may be writing a travelogue, a novel or a book of essays but certain heartfelt ideas prod him on. The thought content of his books is mighty. You will not find big, long passages full of abstractions in his books. The incidents, the characters and the places convey thoughts and feelings. It is marvellous, simply lovely to see this man work book after book. He has been true to his ideas, true to himself.

He does not shun away from commenting on politics, wars, economy and other worldly affairs. That way, Ghosh has not been very diplomatic. Had he joined a lobby, he might have gone places as many of his better-known co-professionals have done. But no, so far Ghosh has shown remarkable sincerity.

The Circle of Reason, as the name suggests is a book written in defense of reason, logic and rationality. In practical situations, logic hardly works. Cause and effect is not a practical theory. In a laboratory, it may be that the reaction of mixing two substances can be predicted. But it is not so in real life. Especially, India is a place where irrationality is pursued almost like a religion. Superstitions, blind beliefs, prejudices, the dominance of the supernatural in the collective psyche hardly allow any fresh thinking. As a child is born, slowly but surely she/he is taken into the cult of the illogical. Investigation, first hand exposure and experience are not allowed. *The Circle of Reason* is a revolt against this trend. I am saying this even at the risk of over-simplifying matters. To a new reader, it may not look so at the first reading. But if we think about the idea behind the novel, we will certainly recognise rationality as the driving force of this apparently irrationally structured novel. As a thinking Indian, Ghosh is bothered about the unhygienic conditions prevailing in the country. What is the use of Ganga Jal as a purifying agent when Ganga itself has gone so dirty? Carbolic acid may be a better purifying agent. So we have 'havan samagri' being pasted in carbolic acid.

Colonisation, recolonisation, neo colonisation and decolonisation are recurring thoughts in Ghosh's work. Ghosh compulsively turns to this perspective. In this novel also the monopoly of England over cloth market is pointed out. India and her spirit have been crushed by British domination. A new kind of thinking order is required which assimilates both traditional Indian views with Western sense of rationality. But then 'traditional Indian view' may not prove to be a very simple thing. So many folds exist within the Indian view that to take the Sanskrit Brahminical cult as the authentic representative of it will lead us to new wrongs. This plurality is also the richness of Indian thought. What is required is a proper recognition of this intellectual diversity and its thorough study. At the same time the Western trends need not be shunted away. But I do not know whether Ghosh implies all this or my own view has intervened.

Admirers of Ghosh agree that *The Shadow Lines* is his best book so far. I also share this opinion. What should one say about this book? It is moving. It is appealing. It affects you. It becomes your own story at some point or the other. It strikes a universal chord. At the level of reflection, it offers many suggestions. It proposes so many tentative opinions to the reader. To me, the most outstanding thought of this book seems to be its firm establishment of adulthood in its origin i.e. childhood. Adulthood is important in itself, no doubt. It has immense capacity to evolve, to grow and emancipate. But there is or there should be a logical connection between the initial stages of life and its later stages. Any psychologically well-grown person needs this connectivity. We live our childhood. We recall it. We also recreate it for our convenience, for our children, and for our graceful life-story. Whatever we may do with it but we should be wired to it. Somehow an individual's growth should be honestly drawn before herself/ himself. If we are not clear about ourselves, we can not be clear about the world. This seems to me the most important contribution this book makes at the level of thought. The narrator as well as other characters so naturally spring up from their childhood, to adolescence and then to adulthood. You can always recognise a character. This is also because the book is about sincere people. There are persons in the real world who are so worldly wise, such experts in manipulative intrigues, so completely devoid of trust that it becomes impossible to view their childhood. But I will call the birth of this scoundrellike personality an unhealthy development forced by over exposure to the negative side of the world. If telling lies is maturity, *The Shadow Lines* does not have mature characters. Not that all characters are saints. No, not that but their flaws are human, explicable and again rooted to their past. For me, it is a master-stroke of Ghosh at the art of characterisation. In very simple words, a child is there in all adults. It should be visible also at times. Total severing of a person from the child in her/him will lead to complete loss of simplicity and faith in human goodness, qualities essential for positive living.

There are so many other viewpoints in this book. Commonly the most important idea drawn from this book is the shallowness of international borders, lines of control, frontiers and boundaries. Ultimately it is all in the mind. Through the description of the pain of partition, riots and communal hatred Ghosh drives home the idea of unreal borders. There is no substance in such strict borders. In his later books, we shall see the author's yearning for the good old Middle Ages when free trade existed between India and so many other countries. India was a geographical entity cut out by nature herself. Artificial borders did not exist. Barbed wires, fencing and patrolling were not required. All this was changed in a day— the day Vasco de Gama set his foot on the Indian soil. Western classification, division and demarcation had arrived.

Matters of heart, love and relationships form a major part of this story. Keen insights are provided into these affairs. The Indian middle class and its defensive mentality are also described. The author is somehow on the reader's side. He does not disappoint at all. The book meets our expectations.

As has been suggested *In An Antique Land* is a book written to recall the spirit of a world that no longer exists. The love that once existed between a Tunician Jewish merchant and an Indian tribal is overwhelming. It makes us sorry for our world of terrorism, riots and communal discord. This is a well-researched book based on old records and the author's tireless investigation.

In *The Calcutta Chromosome* Ghosh has tried to give an answer to West's monopoly over scientific discoveries and inventions. He has tried to deconstruct the aura around Ronald Ross, the British scientist who found the cause of malaria. This is perhaps the most daring work by this author. He breaks literary traditions. At times it looks like science fiction. But the driving logic remains to undo the Western sense of superiority.

Dancing in Cambodia, At Large in Burma gives impetus to decolonisation in its own way. The book proves just one thing—the coloniser or the dictator cannot kill a people. Even in impossible situations civilisations and culture and the spirit of a people survive and live. In this sense, the book is very satisfying. A nation lives in its culture and art and not in governments.

Countdown comes as a kind of shock to those who have gone used to Ghosh's pro-India, anti-West stand. In this book, Ghosh exposes the Indian and the Pakistani nuclear lobbies. Nuclearisation is not going to solve anything. It is just a trick to divert people's attention from the real problems of their lives. With ever-plunging living standards and disappearing civic amenities nuclear explosion is a kind of mass-dream with which the people are expected to forget their plight.

In *The Glass Palace*, we find our old Amitav Ghosh again. This is basically a book about European greed and the cruelty of colonisation. It is an intricate novel that covers almost three generations. It has many driving ideas. The British came to rich lands like India and Burma with an unsatiable greed and drained them of all resources. The royal families suffered most. The kings and queens were reduced to puppets. With the end of the royal way of life, a whole idea of sumptuousness died. Luxury, connoisseurship and abundance ended. An alluring face of human existence was damaged. The ruthless cutting of jungles through systematised, mechanical ways feels so cruel.

For me, this is also a book about human contradictions. Any human being cannot be fully explained. No one's behaviour can be totally predicted, no matter how sharp your perceptions may be. The characters take a U-turn in this novel. The element of surprise keeps the reader hooked. Raj Kumar is fascinated by Dolly. But he also ditches her. Uma mourns her husband's death but she also behaves in a loose manner. Queen Supayalat is a terrible dictator but she punishes herself with a life of exile for the love for her husband. Alison loves Dinu but she also goes with Arjun. Characters take you by surprise. In this sense, this novel is more life-like, more practical. The ability of an adult to change her/his behaviour has been accepted here. The mediocrity, meanness and weakness of human nature have been acknowledged.

For a regular reader, the books by Amitav Ghosh provide a delicious feast. Together, they present a way of looking at the world. They provide a perspective. Many things are clarified. Many matters are thought out. So many intricacies of human life have been revealed. As readers, we cannot help admiring the immense capacity of this man to create his own world.

2
The Circle of Reason

Many big changes go quietly unnoticed. The first novel by Amitav Ghosh, *The Circle of Reason* brought one such change. *The Circle of Reason* is remarkable for many reasons. Its theme is different from traditional concerns of Indian English Fiction. It challenges a direct and simple appreciation. In fact, it needs a different type of approach to be grasped fully. The book itself is sort of a paradox. It exuberates restlessness with extreme control and poise. The new thrust and lift that came to Indian English Fiction during late eighties and early nineties is partly due to this pathbreaking work. It internationalized our fiction. It brought a refreshing contemporareity. It is daring in its experimentation with the form, content and language of the novel.

The novel, although not strictly organized, is episodic in nature. In this sense it can be called picaresque. The novel is a journey from *Sattva* to *Rajas* to *Tamas*, the three parts of the novel. As we can see the journey is lopsided. Traditionally the protagonist Alu should have gone from 'Tama' (darkness) to 'Satwa' (purity). As we will see in the coming pages, Amitav Ghosh freely mixes past, present and future in his books. So he does in this book. He writes in a chain of thoughts. He describes one incident and if the incident links itself to any past happening, he immediately goes to that past incident. So the whole fabric of the novel keeps floating, going backward and forward. And this is quite logical in its own way. In any case present is born out of past. So why should one not go to the great reservoir of memories, dreams and desires *i.e.*, past.

The novel is crowded with characters. The episodes are only loosely connected. Alu is the only constant factor who lives a life by trial and error method; falls at times, stands up again and finally moves on to realise his potential, if he has any. The novel, without becoming a morbid case-history, underlines the troubled times, through which all of us are living. Like a typical open-ended novel, it ends without providing readymade solutions. There is a soothing effect at the end. Different threads seem to draw together yet there is no effort at preaching. In a typical picaresque fashion, Alu moves from Lalpukar in India to Al-Ghazira in Egypt and then to a small town in the northeastern edge of Algerian Sahara. The journey does not bring any kind of satisfaction or success. It celebrates the sense of unquiet wanderings. It goes on and on searching a vision suitable for present times. It is like chasing a phantom that ultimately vanishes into the thin air.

The Circle of Reason has both historical as well as mythological elements. Mythical references have been moulded to reflect contemporary conditions in a true new historicist fashion. Girish Karnad is another man to have done so, so successfully in his plays. Here, Ghosh weaves ideas, characters and metaphors through magic and irony and develops his fictional motifs. Characters are not far from metaphors; they become metaphors. The characters as well as different situations of the novel stand for rootlessness. As a critic, I often wonder at our fascination about the idea of rootlessness. The present literati seems obsessed with the idea of migration. Migration, diasporic feelings, rootlessness and a new kind of sensibility born out of these factors—these things are unique to our age. Since the beginning of the human race, migration has been a major phenomena. But that migration used to be in huge groups. The Aryans leaving Central Asia and spreading across Asia and Europe was no solitary act. The whole race migrated! What is new, typical and unique of our age is loneliness and sense of vacuum that comes with individual migration or migration of comparatively smaller groups. Since time immemorial, the human race has been obsessed with ideas of belonging, heritage, clan, inheritance and native soil. Now we are surprised at our own condition. We want to sing our own songs—songs of estrangement, dissociation and withdrawal. Suddenly everyone has become an emigrant—a village student in a nearby town, a semi-urbanite at Delhi or Mumbai, a Punjabi in Bengal, a Tamilian in Orissa, an Asian in Europe and so on. Everyone is away from the roots—where have all the roots gone?

There is nothing in this novel that can ordinarily be called a home. Significantly, it is initially located in a refugee village. It only settles the human race temporarily as a refugee on this planet. It goes back and forth to Bangladesh and Calcutta. Then it reaches the Middle East via Kerala. The last location again significantly is that of a desert with shifting sand dunes. The story moves in an uncertain atmosphere. One is never sure whether it's a city or a village. Even the ideas are not stable; they keep us shaking. Even the most basic element of coherence, time, is not arranged normally. *The Circle of Reason* can only be called an endless saga of restlessness, uncertainty and change.

The novel basically tells three stories. The first part deals with the story of Balram. He is a rationalist and is influenced by the life of Louis Pasteur. He is idealistic to the extent of being inhuman. He has no involvement with people. He treats others simply as objects of observation and/or change. He takes his whims to extreme and becomes self-destructive. In fact, he meets his own mettle in Bhudeb Roy. He is equally cynical. He is a Congressman. Alu, the protagonist, is a nephew of Balram. He is the only one to survive in the family. The second part of the novel tells another tale. An earthly, practical and zestful trader tries to bring together the community of Indians in the Middle East. But again these efforts prove to be unrealistic. The third part is the story of Mrs. Verma, who outrightly rejects rational thinking. She again tries her hand at creating Indian model of community life in the desert. However Alu, Zindi and Jyoti Das, a police officer leave Mrs. Verma and her experiments in the desert. At the end of the novel, these three are in search of newer horizons, unformed hopes and ideas. Hope is their only asset.

The relationship between Alu and Jyoti is not normal. Jyoti, as a police officer, initially views Alu as an extremist. She has her eyes on him right from the first part. Their story is the main source of continuity in this novel. Their relationship also adds thrill. Nevertheless, since the basic building block of their interaction is officialdom and power of the state, it lacks human warmth. We can see this relationship as a comment on present day man-woman encounter which lacks natural elements and is totally artificial at times.

The story begins when an eight-year-old orphan Nachiketa Bose comes to live with his uncle Balram Bose in Lalpukar. His rickshaw is chased by Boloi da. Boloi da runs a cycle repair shop and eagerly utilises every opportunity of enjoyment. The only remarkable thing about this orphan is his extraordinary head. It is 'an extraordinary head, huge, several times too large for an eight year old, and curiously uneven, bulging all over with knots and bumps' (3). While everyone is busy in comparing the head with other suitable objects and bring it in a perspective, it is Boloi da, who gives Alu his life long name as well as part of his identity, 'No, it's not like a rock at all. It's an Alu, a potato, a huge, freshly dug, lumpy potato. So Alu he was named and Alu he was to remain' (3). On an allegorical plane Alu is someone rooted in soil and therefore in identity. But as we will see by his torturous wandering, Alu seems only to satirize his name.

Balram is a freak. He claims to be a rationalist. He admires scientists like Jagdish Bose, Meghnad Saha and above every one else Louis Pasteur. They are his ideals. He is obsessed with the science of phrenology. Phrenology is the study of the size and shape of people's heads in the belief that you can find out about their characters and abilities from this. Needless to add that Alu becomes a curious case study for Balram. Balram applies his instrument for measuring heads on Alu, much to Alu's woes. Slowly he gets used to it. Balram is determined to match 'outside' of a person with his 'inside.'

Alu settles in Lalpukar, but his troubles do not. He is admitted to Bhudeb Roy's school. Roy's son Gopal bullies Alu and finally Alu is forced to leave school. Shombhu Debnath is a lowly man in Lalpukar. It is not exactly respectable to learn weaving from him. Yet, Alu does the same. This gives the novelist an opportunity to give a historical perspective to the skill of weaving. Ghosh is eloquent about the past value of weaving: 'Man at the loom is the finest example of mechanical man [...] it has created not separate worlds but one, for it has never permitted the division of the world. The loom recognizes no continents and no countries. It has tied the world together with its bloody ironies from the beginning of human time [...]. Human beings have woven and traded in cloth from the time they built their first houses and cities. Indian cloth was found in the graves of the pharaohs. Indian soil is strewn with cloth from China. The whole of the ancient world hummed with the cloth trade. The silk route from China, running through Central Asia and Persia to the ports of the Mediterranean and from there to the markets of Africa and Europe, bound continents together for more centuries than we can count.

India first gave cotton, Gossypium Indicus, to the world. The cities of the Indus Valley grew cotton as early as 1500 B.C. But soon cotton was busy spinning its web around the world. It had king Sennacherib of Mesopotamia in its toils by 700 B.C. and before long it had found its way to Herodotus in Greece [...].

When the history of the world broke, cotton and cloth were behind it [...] the machine had driven men mad [...]. Lancashire poured out its waterfalls of cloth and the once cloth hungry and peaceful Englishmen and Dutchmen and Danes of Calcutta,

Chandanagar, Madras, and Bombay turned their trade a garrote to make every continent safe for the cloth of Lancashire [...]. Millions of Africans and half of America were enslaved by cotton. And then weaving changed mechanical man again with the computer. In the mid-nineteen century when Charles Babbage built his first calculating machine, using the principles of storing information on punched cards, he took his idea not from systems of writing or from mathematics, but from the draw-loom. The Chinese have used punched cards to discriminate between warp threads in the weaving of silk since 1000 B.C. [...].

It is a gory history in parts, a story of greed and destruction. Every scrap of cloth is stained by a bloody past. But it is the only history we have and history is hope as well as despair (56-58).

Here is a true Bengali singing the greatness of loom and cotton and weaving. We know what cotton weaving means to people of Bengal. But more importantly, it is the interpretation of history that is to be noted. First Ghosh divides man as mechanical man and the other type can be easily assumed, thinking man. Those who have gone through Emerson's *American Scholar* know 'the man, thinking.' This division is only to underline the basic faculties of men and women. Emerson explaining the sordid state of affairs, says, 'Man is thus metamorphosed into a thing, into many things. The planter who is man sent out into the field to gather food, is seldom cheered by any idea of the true dignity of his ministry. He sees his bushel and his cart and nothing beyond and sinks into the farmer, instead of Man on the farm. The tradesman scarcely ever gives an ideal worth to his work, but is ridden by the routine of his craft, and the soul is subject to dollars. The priest becomes a form; the attorney a statute-book; the mechanic a machine; the sailor a rope of the ship' (*An Anthology of American Literature of the Nineteenth Century*, Euresian Publishing House, New Delhi).

In his thinking, Ghosh, as we will see, is talking about the Man on the loom or even further the idea behind the loom and not just the instrument. It is also the idea behind history. Loom united human race at times; it divided at others; it brought victories to some, subjugation to others. This passage is significant in its historical perspective, simply because the author here goes not to mere events or states of being but to themes that run them. The anti-colonial note against the monopoly of Lancashire cloth is obvious. Then the relation of loom to computer, the most advanced achievement of Man at Machine, is beautifully and factually established. The link between storing information in the form of dots in a punched card and the intricate structure of loom and its functioning is very clearly established. This is exactly what historians mean when they say that all history is history of ideas. Ideas are the guiding forces that run both men and their actions. The keen eye does not stop with events or states of being/conditions but goes on to search the whys and hows. The job of the scholar is to arrange information and knowledge input in a systematic and logical pattern. Anyone can say as to what happened and when but only the intellectual can tell why it happened, what shaped the event and how it took place. Only the man thinking can synthesise the whole gamut of unrelated chaotic past into a perspective. Only then we are able to understand history and its significance. Ghosh is clearly into this process of writing history in the above passage.

Coming back to Alu's story, we see Alu getting feverishly involved in his uncle's plans of cleaning the refugee shanties with carbolic acid. But at the level of human intentions the cleaning operation is aimed against Bhudeb Roy. The movement is to finish germs. But Balram symbolising reason has a natural enemy in Bhudeb Roy who is propagating the personality cult and is engaged in irrational activities. Thus, the movement to finish germs becomes the movement to finish Bhudeb and his types. But events take their own turn. A devastating fire destroys all—Balram, his home and the school. Bhudeb Roy finds in Alu an easy scapegoat. Bhudeb declares Alu a dreaded terrorist. From this point onwards, the dangerous life of Alu begins. He begins to live on the edge, the brink of normality. Jyoti Das, an Assistant Superintendent of Police is told about Alu and his alleged terrorist activities. Alu rushes to Calcutta, from there to Kerala and finally on a boat to Al-Ghazira. All the while he is chased by the police. He even had to give up travelling by buses and trains; he moves through Nilgiri forests. Alu's life is away from the normal. The threat of police constantly enhances the thrill of his adventure. The vagabondish nature of this tale becomes very clear. Besides being a comment on present civilization of rootlessness, the story of Alu also acts as a means for the reader to get adventurous. Settled in the set routine of our lives, Alu's story kindles imagination. Adventure, threat, danger are deep based in human psyche. Alu's story gives us a chance to live or relive that part of our psyche. It is a depiction of a life without centre. Those interested in the deriving nihilistic joys may do a wonderful Derridian analysis of this book. But that is not my cup, certainly not for the present.

Balram personifies reason. How far an action is relevant to the present day situations—this is his only parameter for judging things and individuals. Reason juxtaposed with religion, provides a full-length debate in this novel. Balram is fascinated by the book, *Life of Pasteur*. Pasteur is his ideal, logic his God. Rational thinking is his only goal in life. But the author is mature enough to point out the end of rationality in practical situations. Scientific temper, the cause and effect theory do not work in real situations. Balram's case is that of firmness of logic. He cannot look beyond reason. It should be so rationally and so it must be for him. He cannot accept a hair breadth's difference from the upright, straight, unchangeable logical path. That is why Balram's plans are invariably put out of gear when put into practice. The story begins with his childhood. He wanted to study science and emulate great scientists like Pasteur and Jagdish Bose. But his teachers in Dhaka decide that he's good for history and direct him to Dr. Radhakrishnan, the teacher of Philosophy at Presidency College, Calcutta.

There at Calcutta, his favourite pass time is to study heads. Many times he faces trouble due to his compulsive, habit of studying and commenting on others' heads. But Balram is made of stiff stuff. His uncompromising stand on rationality as the only theory of life wins him a life-long friend, Gopal. He also gets associated with a rationalist society. But Gopal, even though his best friend senses something wrong, 'As he watched Balram go, Gopal had a premonition: a premonition of the disaster he would call upon himself and all of them, if ever he is allowed to take charge of the society. He decided then, with an uncharacteristic determination, that he would do everything in his power to keep that from happening' (50). Quite similarly Balram's wife also senses foul and puts his books on fire. Alu is able to save just one book—*Life of Pasteur*. *Life of Pasteur* is a significant symbol in this novel. But before going to that, let us see how cleverly Ghosh has put prophecy and rationality side by side. Rationality of Balram is juxtaposed with the premonition of his well wishers—contradictory forces are at work. Isn't it a pattern of life itself? Life cannot be defined as black or white. Ghosh is a good writer because his works provide balanced views of contradictory elements. Premonition comes true but rationality does not die, either. Inspired by this book, Balram starts a school in his village called 'School of Reason.' This is the ultimate test of his long cherished dreams of reason. Toru Debi teaches sewing and Shombhu Debnath, weaving. For the time being Balram and Bhudeb with their opposing obsessions come to a common point—serving society with the tool of education. But this is a short lived and temporary phase. Soon the conflict between them reaches the boiling point. But *Life of Pasteur* survives the crisis and goes on its journey to Al-Ghazira with Alu.

The role played by the book is quite intricate. When Alu is first introduced to the book (and we too in the process), Balram is worried about Alu's lack of response. He lectures Alu with animated passion. Alu listens to him with 'wide-eyed silence.' Balram is touched. He reads from the book and stops to see tears in Alu's eyes. And when Alu retrieves the book from fire, it is Balram's turn to be wet-eyed. So the book exists as a bond between uncle and nephew—an extension of the tradition of reason from one generation to the other. The greatest win for a rationalist is to win over someone else on her/his side.

This rationality wages a war against germs, which are the root of all diseases. The analogy can easily be taken further where carbolic acid as a tool of scientific temper tries to finish diseases, and rationality as the thought offshoot of scientific temper tries to end the ills of society. The cleansing mechanisms in different forms run as a metaphor throughout the novel. In Al-Ghazira Hajji Fahmy makes Adil and his cousin bathe in antiseptic. Carbolic acid is very much part and parcel of Alu's cleaning programme. Towards the end of the novel, Mrs. Verma is shown using carbolic acid instead of Ganga Jal. Dr. Mishra remarks, 'Carbolic acid has become holy water' (411). To this Mrs. Verma retorts, 'What does it matter whether it is Ganga Jal or Carbolic acid? It is just a question of cleaning the place, isn't it? People thought something was clean once, now they think something else is clean. What difference does it make to the dead, Dr. Mishra?' (411). Ghosh is of course pointing out to the blind faith of millions of Indians in Ganga Jal even though the water of the life giving river is so badly polluted.

In fact, the book, *Life of Pasteur* is related to Mrs. Verma's life also. Her father introduced her to the book and it was because of it only she became a microbiologist. The story of the book comes to an end only when Kulfi, defying all efforts by Balram and Alu, dies. It is a defeat of reason because the course of action does not go on rational lines. The book itself states, '... without the germ life would become impossible because death would be incomplete' (396).

Alu's real name is Nachiketa. As with everything else of Amitav Ghosh, the choice of this mythological name has a meaning. Nachiketa, in mythology is the boy who waits at

Yama's doors in obedience to his father. Waiting at Yama's doors naturally means waiting at the door of death. Nachiketa is sage Uddalaka's son. Nachiketa is known for his perseverance. In his pursuit of true knowledge of Brahman, Nachiketa incurs his father's displeasure. In a fit of rage, Uddalaka curses Nachiketa to go and suffer in the nether world *i.e.* Yamaloka (the world of the death god Yama). Yama, on his part, is also the embodiment of righteousness. His work is such that he just can not afford to be unjust. Nachiketa sincerely pleads to Yama to give him divine knowledge. He wins Yama's heart by his commitment to the chosen cause. He receives the knowledge about the true nature of Brahman (Bramha gyan) from Yama. Nachiketa's single-mindedness is coupled with disinterested action. He is not working for getting something. As the myth goes the young sage is lured by Yama by the pleasures of heaven. Nachiketa refuses to go to heaven. As he has learnt the true nature of being he knows Brahman is all pervading. Moreover Agni (fire) is a purifying agent. Fire, even in hell, does the work of cleansing. Here the myth begins to connect with our story. Carbolic acid is also a purifying agent. At Kulfi's death, paste for puja is made of carbolic acid instead of ghee. At times, I feel, *The Circle of Reason* is simply a response of Amitav Ghosh to the unhygienic conditions of India. It is a complex response of the author to appalling dirt and filth in a land whose people have always talked of purity of soul as well as surroundings. The contradiction is fascinating. People insist on taking morning baths, purifying their homes with havans (fire) and keep fasts for internal cleansing. And still, they turn a blind eye to all the garbage and dirt in their holy rivers and holy places. The mythical Nachiketa might have been interested in big things. Alu's concern is simply how to overcome germ, and disease.

Nachiketa Bose (Alu) also waits at death's door when in Al-Ghazira he is buried alive when a building collapses. Without food and water, for days together, he does one thing and that is thinking. He knows the truth to be present in scientific reasoning. He wants to apply the scientific approach in removing the ills of present day society. When he finally comes out, Alu declares that money is the enemy of mankind for 'it travels on every man and every woman, silently preparing them for their defeat,' turning one against the other (281).

Out of the multiple layers of narrative in this novel, one layer seems committed to the cause of education. How should our children be educated? What should they be taught? Education is one big question that haunts the author. Education is memorization of facts at one level. At another, it is a tool to get a livelihood. At yet another, it sharpens human sensitivities. It kindles social consciousness in children. Can education uplift living standards of Indian masses and save them from nightmarish depths of poverty, ignorance and disease? Balram, a schoolteacher, acts as Ghosh's mouthpiece when he says, 'It would be wrong; it would be immoral. Children go to school for their first glimpse into the life of the mind. Not for jobs. If I thought that my teaching is nothing but a means of finding jobs; I'd stop teaching tomorrow' (52). So, 'glimpse into the life of mind' is all that education should do. It seems so far from our real burdensome curricula for children? Where is the pleasure in education? Ghosh seems to suggest a pattern where children are trained on rational patterns. They may enjoy their training. Their curiosity is not suffocated by authority. Their natural impulse to ask questions is encouraged. They are trained to find their own answers. Ghosh's idea of education becomes more clear when he deals with Louis Pasteur's life and education.

Pasteur's life exemplifies the fact that education should be aimed at answering the common every-day problems of people. Bread alone is not the answer. Several other forms of thinking are needed to be really useful to society. Pasteur's father was a poor tanner. The young Pasteur's laboratory was life itself. He did not come to science by thinking about the nature of existence and atom. He actually left the study of crystallography in order to answer the most common problem of brewers of France. 'What was it that made bear rot?' This is how he came to discover the infinitesimally small germ and the good and harm it causes to human life. Life, therefore, is the best teacher. Experience and exposure to real life situations are more crucial than classroom instruction. Education is for life but better education is from life. As Shombhu Debnath says, 'Skill is not enough; you have all that you ever will. Technique is just the beginning. The world is your challenge now; look around you and see if your loom can encompass' (88).

Amitav Ghosh is a writer who is never vary of making comments on politics and power equations within India. In an environment of internationalization and globalization, 'restlessness' is only too natural. On one hand, there is the traditional and perhaps 'out-dated' group of people who are obsessed with colonization of India by the British and decolonization of what the British did. But Ghosh's focus is also on recolonization and neo-colonization of the globe by multinational companies. The tools of Balram for self-reliance are carbolic acid, loom and sewing machine. We are reminded of Gandhi's Charakha. The situation today may be post-colonial but Ghosh effectively shows how socialism and democracy have been betrayed in this land. Ghosh, throughout his career as a writer shows a love-hate relationship with decolonisation. At times he is angered by the harm and insults given by colonisers and yet at other times, he is unsparing in his attack on hypocrisy and lack of sincerity of the colonised. At one point Mrs. Verma shouts at Mishra, 'Who sabotaged Lohia? Don't think we've forgotten—we've seen you wallowing filth with the Congress, while high theory drips from your mouth, we've heard you spouting about the misery of masses, while, your fingers dig into their pockets' (380). Even the mechanics of organizing political meetings is not spared. The politicians are not sincere, nor are they charismatic any longer. They hire workers and through them an audience is arranged. Bhudeb in shameless political exhibitionism holds a meeting under the banyan tree. His men have gathered people from the entire village. But Balram, the man of reason, is bent upon disrupting the meeting. Even without sufficient volunteers he manages to disturb the meeting with buckets full of carbolic acid. On the other hand Bhudeb's sons and henchmen hang his life size poster on the tree. Ghosh here subtly fingers the coming 'advertising' culture of Indian politics. It also points towards successful running of several dynasties within the so-called democratic set up of the country.

The Circle of Reason makes an unconventional reading. The form of the novel may be taken to symbolize the chaotic state of today's society. But the parallel can be taken only to a certain limit because howsoever unorthodox, the novel does have plot, theme and characterisation. The effect that it produces is not at all chaotic.

The novel seems to suggest that everything is actually a matter of how we look at it. Attitudes matter. History is not unchangeable; it very much gets moulded by the way we look at it. Time in this novel is characterized by remarkable fluidity. The lives that this novel depicts are all lived on the brink of abnormality. These are dangerously lived lives driven by focused passions. The characters are uncompromising. And this is something quite common I have noticed among worthy writers. Their characters do not compromise. They are mostly talented people given to their specific causes. The fire within them may not be visible at times; but it is always there. Somehow adjustment, compromise and worldly wisdom seem to stand for mediocrity for these writers. Ghosh also builds his extraordinary tale with the help of extraordinary characters.

REFERENCE

Ghosh, Amitav. 1986. *The Circle of Reason*. London: Himash Hamilton.

3
The Shadow Lines

All criticism is personal or at least that is what I feel. Right from choice of an author, or a book, how it works on one's mind, how one takes it, adjusts and balances its impressions on one's mind and finally how one comments on it—it is all terribly personal. *The Shadow Lines* has been no ordinary experience for me. It brings a ticklish, sad, sweet sensation with it. It is difficult to comment on this book just because it is so good. Many papers have been written on it. It has received the Sahitya Academy Award way back in 1989. But I am not going to talk about the rich technical structure of this book, or mixing of past, present and future in this book. What I am going to do is much simpler but at the same time very difficult—I will try to answer one question in the coming pages—why does the book affect the reader so much? I wish to say all the things that I like in this novel. By the way, I have not disliked anything in it.

To begin with, let us talk about the sweet, sad sensation that the book arouses. You just cannot keep back your smile as you go through the pages. The book is written on an emotional plane, underlining and explaining the small, universal truths of life. Fascinatingly true depiction of the mental condition of children is so remarkable. The author, it seems, has relived his childhood in this book. On a psychological plane, the book roots personality and identity in childhood. The narrator stands out as an adult rooted in his childhood experiences. Whenever he experiences life, his reaction to it stems out of his childhood impressions. How does he take cities like London, Calcutta or Dhaka or people like his cousin Ila, or acquaintances like May and Nick—everything springs from his childhood perceptions. It seems so natural. It seems the only honest way of taking life and its experiences. So, if I may take the conventional critical term, childhood is a major theme of this book. The treatment of the subject is simply overwhelming. Tridib is the narrator's older cousin. His impact on the narrator's life is immense. Tridib and the narrator-child have a special bond. They have in a way, conspired to look at the world with their own eyes or rather Tridib's eccentric, rational, detached eyes. When Tridib tells the narrator about his childhood at London, the child-narrator tries to imagine Tridib as a small child. He tries hard but cannot imagine Tridib as a small boy and finally 'I had decided he had looked like me' (3). So while listening stories of London, Cairo, and other exotic places, the narrator travels, identifying himself completely with the bigger, (almost perfect to his child's eyes) role model. The narrator's identification with his hero *i.e.*, Tridib is so intense that when asked for a response, the narrator says 'I was nervous now: I could see that he (Tridib) was waiting to hear what I'd have to say and I didn't want to disappoint him' (28). Thus, begins his training at looking at things by Tridib's standards. It is not that Tridib is trying to bulldoze his presence on the narrator. In the area where the narrator lives, Gariahat and Gole Park in Calcutta, Tridib is very well known on the streets. All pan shop owners, sweet shop owners, boys on the street know Tridib because the place is his favourite 'adda' or 'haunt,' we may say in English. The narrator is enveloped in the protective presence of Tridib, 'I [...] was grateful for the small privileges his presence secured for me on those streets: For the odd sweet given to me by a shopkeeper of his acquaintance; For being rescued from a fight in the park by some young fellow who knew him' (8). The narrator has a pure child-like love for Tridib. As a child he bursts with pride at Tridib's show of intellect and superior knowledge on those roadside haunts. The narrator's sense of pride expands when Tridib treats him like an equal, an adult and shares secrets with him. He fiercely defends Tridib when people ridicule him on his back for all his made-up or real wonder stories. The child in the narrator is so dominant that when years later May, Tridib's beloved, spots him in London in the crowd after her performance in an orchestra 'suddenly she smiled, rose on tiptoe, pulled my head down and kissed me on my cheeks' (15). He is an adult here, treated as a child.

Great fiction, I have noticed, always patterns itself on psychological truths. Sometimes I wonder whether these great novelists really smuggle the psychological precepts directly from texts of psychology. For example, castration fear in male children is a major childhood theme in psychoanalytical literature. Tridib encashes this while telling a story to the narrator and his younger brother Robi, 'He (Tridib) had smiled and gone on to tell us in ghastly detail about the circumcision rites of one of the desert tribes. And then, spectacles glinting, he had said: So before you leave you'd better decide whether you would care to have all that done to your little wee-wees, just in case you're captured' (19). Another psychological truth that Ghosh successfully demonstrates is accumulation of complexes in childhood and growing years. Rich and influential relatives in the form of Mayadebi, Shaheb and Ila come to middle class household of the narrator. To add to it, they come from different parts of the world with strange tales. The complex is so deep rooted in the narrator that he cannot think of these big relatives as blood relation. He says, 'I would not bring myself to believe that their worth in my eyes could be reduced to something so arbitrary and unimportant as a blood relationship' (3). This can be taken as clue to the narrator's unsuccessful relationship with Ila. He reduces himself so much in his own eyes that Ila never actually notices him except of course, after she has permanently damaged herself by marrying Nick. The narrator loves Ila but he cannot say so. He is in awe of her. The inequality of their needs arises out of his sense of small worth. She introduces him to Nick as a child and immediately he heaps it on himself as another feather in his complexive cap. It is almost painful to see him as a child falling a prey to inferiority complex. Ila says, 'He's very big. Much bigger than you: much stronger too. He's twelve, three years older than us' (49). After these words of Ila, life never remains the same for the narrator, 'after that day Nick Price, whom I had never seen [...] became a spectral presence beside me in my looking glass; growing with me, but always bigger and better, and in some way more desirable—I did not know what, except that it was so in Ila's eyes and therefore true' (50).

The narrator's fascination for Ila is well known to everyone in the family. As a child he gulps humiliation when his mother exposes his obsession with Ila's expected visit to India. The child is exposed as being vulnerable before Ila's charms. Ila comes to know early in life that the narrator needs her, not she him. It is an unequal relationship, right from the beginning and the origin very much lies in the narrator's middle class background.

It is not that these descriptions of childhood are fraught with pain only. In fact, some pain is part of every stage of life. Ila's pain is that Nick ignores her. No one's situation is perfect and that is life. Some pages beautifully fill us with childhood joys, 'I pushed her (Ila), urging her on, my belly churning with a breathless hide and seek excitement' (46).

Another subtle aspect of childhood is specific world of the girl child. It is lovely. Girls and their eternal longing for beauty and home are delicately picturised. Girls equate beauty with desirability and acceptance. Ila tells her own sad experience at school in London where Nick does not come to help her. She narrates it through her doll's name, Magda. Ila and the narrator are playing house-house and Magda is their child. Magda, their little kid, has gone to school and everyone is struck by Magda's beauty. We may easily read Ila in place of Magda because it is her own failure to get Nick's attention that she is actually narrating, 'you couldn't blame them for staring: they'd never seen anyone as beautiful as Magda.' And her very next sentence links beauty in a girl to her popularity and likeability, 'And they liked her too: they all wanted to be friends with her—girls, boys, and teachers, all of them' (73). It is the eternal feminine datum that beauty gets you everything, just everything. This game also tells about the urge of children to grow up, be adults, play Mamma and Papa and for once be in the controlling, guiding position.

When we see the world through the eyes of the narrator-child, we come to realise their worries as well. Nothing frightens kids more than anxiety and agitation in adults; adults are expected to hold their world together. When May is expected at Railway station, Tridib gets nervous. 'Tridib was less sanguine now; he was beginning to bite his fingernails. I (narrator-child) was close to tears' (104).

Another rare peep into child-psychology comes when the child-narrator gets to know that Tridib had died. Tridib was very close to him, his friend, philosopher and guide. His influence on the narrator as a child was absolutely absolute. Yet when he listens of his death, 'I felt nothing—no shock, no grief. I did not understand that I would never see him again; my mind was not large enough to accommodate so complete an absence' (239). In our lives also, when children for the first time ask, 'what is dying' or 'why Dadaji or Naniji is lying like that' or 'why are you crying,' we do not know what to say. We do not realize that children do not know what is meant by death.

The mention of Tridib's death brings us to him. He is such a unique character that again it is difficult to limit him with adjectives. He is a good student. He is eccentric. He is tricky. He is a loafer. He is sincere. He is all these and much more. But above everything else he is the man who gave the narrator the keen ability to perceive things, to go for minute and relevant details, to build his own world, to see places and not just visit them, to 'know' people and not just meet them. Tridib has a special kind of presence. Positively or negatively, he has the capacity to affect people. The narrator's grandmother, Tha'mma is almost scared of Tridib's influencing quality, '[...] my grandmother would not let him stay long. She believed him to be capable of exerting his influence at a distance, like a baneful planet' (5). At another point, the narrator declares, 'But even a child I could tell she didn't pity him at all—she feared him.' He has something for everyone—tips for examinations to students, or tips on how to face an interview to a shaken candidate and things like that. He also misuses his power. Once he tells a young man to go to interview dressed in a dhoti because the firm had been taken over by an orthodox 'marvari.' When, the boy does so, he is not allowed within the firm's premises! And yet Tridib is always above the mundane, the common and the ordinary. As the narrator realises he comes to these roadside haunts just to distract himself after exhaustive studies. Tridib's currency is his unpredictability. No one knows where she/he stands with him. He is a bundle of contradictions. In any case Tha'mma's plans to keep the narrator out of Tridib's orbit fail. The narrator drops at Tridib's home on and off escaping school or tuition. Tridib tells him all the stories, his stay in England and the experiences in instalments. The narrator receives every bit of Tridib's influence happily. He literally shapes the narrator's vision. The whole process of training the narrator is deliberate on Tridib's part and spontaneous on the narrator's part, '[...] among other things Tridib was an archaeologist, he was not interested in fairy lands: the one thing he wanted to teach me, he used to say, was to use my imagination with precision' (24). His impact is so substantial that when the narrator visits England he feels captive to Tridib's perceptions.

Tridib's relationship with May is essentially tragic. They are attracted to each other. He writes a highly provocative letter to her. But May is hooked by this man who could write a pornographic letter to her. She comes to India and finds that Tridib is not a monster after all. She finds him lovable. When she first spots him at the railway station, 'He looked awkward, absurdly young, and somehow very reassuring. Also a little funny, because those glasses of his hugely magnified his eyes, and he kept blinking in an anxious embarrassed kind of way. She hadn't been able to help throwing her arms around him; it was just pure relief. She knew at last why she had come and she was glad. It had nothing to do with curiosity' (167). She had come for her love, Tridib.

But May is girl with an extra edge. Her sense of justice, right and wrong is developed. In a very simple explanation to Tridibs death, I wish to say that May's desire to save the weak worked as a catalyst on Tridib's mind when he got out of the Mercedes in Dhaka among rioters to save the old, invalid Jethamoshai. He acts on May's standards, her rule of what is right and what is not. Prior to their visit to Dhaka, while excursing in Calcutta, May forces Tridib to stop his car and saves a dying roadside dog. First Tridib resents but later accepts that she did the right thing and that she need not be apologetic about the inconvenience she caused. Once in Dhaka among frenzied rioteers, May once again cries in horror that they are acting selfishly, saving themselves while endangering Jethamoshai. Tridib gets down to save Jethamoshai and he is cut ear to ear by Muslim rioteers. His end is brutal. May, as she tells the narrator years later, does not realize that she as a white 'mem' was safe but Tridib was their enemy, a Hindu from India. But interpretation cannot stop at material level only. As his name suggests, Tridib is trinity. In an act to save others, he dies. Therefore, he is Jesus. Tridib is the sacrifice of human race at the altar of illogical hatred. Tridib is definitely a prophetic figure. When May saves the stray dog in Calcutta, 'He raised his chin and ran his forefinger down his neck like a barber stropping a razor. Promise me, he said, that you'll do it for me too, if I should ever need it' (174).

Well, May on her part, is on a penance ever since Tridib's death. She sleeps on floor. She fasts. She works for earthquake relief and things like that. She collects money from streets with all her banners, and posters for social welfare. May, like a true disciple of Christ, suffers his death like hell. She is literally on a self-torturing spree. It is only at the very end of the novel she realizes the meaning of sacrifice. She frees herself of her burden of guilt, 'But I know now I didn't kill him; I couldn't have, if I'd wanted. He gave himself up; it was a sacrifice. I know I can't understand it, I know I mustn't try, for any real sacrifice is a mystery' (251-252).

If May is acutely conscious of her duties and faults, Ila is just the opposite, self-absorbed, oblivious of others' needs and irresistibly charming. Ila's portrait is a typical drawing of a modern, beautiful, attractive, foolish girl. She is stubborn. She lives in her own world. She has no sense of commitment as such. Due to lack of depth, she lacks identity. Ila is fluid, flowing and taking different shapes. The narrator comes with a very telling remark on the photos Ila shows him in their childhood, 'But somehow, though Ila could tell me everything about those parties and dances, what she said and what she did and what she wore, she herself was always unaccountably absent in the pictures' (22). The core of Ila's existence in this book is her spell over the narrator. And it is not for nothing. When she comes to meet the narrator at Trafalgar Square, 'she looked up at the church, spotted me and smiled. A couple of tourists standing beside me gasped. She was so improbably, absurdly beautiful, I began to laugh' (18). She turns the narrator crazy. He is helpless before her. It is a repeated pattern in this book. The narrator is again and again defeated by her. He knows his weakness and cannot do anything about it. Ila, on her part, is enthralled by Nick. Nick is white. He is strong and big. So in a sense we can say that Ila's condition in relation to Nick is the same as the narrator's in relation to her. This careless, self-willed, pampered, beautiful girl has actually taken the narrator's life hostage. At one point, when her hurting, ignoring goes beyond limits, 'I felt the tears running down my cheeks' (111). After consoling him a bit, she again goes to Nick and when she does not come back 'I knew she had taken my life hostage yet again; I knew that a part of my life as a human being had ceased: that I no longer existed, but as a chronicle' (112).

Ila is bent upon carrying her self-damaging attraction for undeserving Nick. He is her weakness. She wants him, and fantasizes about him. Finally, she succeeds in getting married to him but the price she pays is heavy indeed. She acts blindly. She cannot see that she is clearly being exploited. Right from the beginning Nick has plans to start a business where Ila's parents are expected to invest (97). Later, as expected, Ila's father purchases a flat for them in London. Even the expenditure for their honeymoon is borne by her father. Mockery is evident in the tone when the narrator describes plans of Ila's parents to buy them a flat, arrange honeymoon and after formal registration of marriage in London, go to Calcutta for 'one of the most lavish weddings' (154). All this fairytale stuff soon ends in Ila's swollen eyes over Nick sleeping with another woman. All her father's aura, rank and money, her own beauty and job turn against her. Her husband gets complexive. Ila tells the narrator, 'He wanted to make a point; to let me know that I shouldn't take anything for granted just because we're living in a flat my father bought for me. And because I have a job and he doesn't't' (188). Poison has already entered their marriage as it normally does into so many marriages. Ila's marriage can be taken as a comment on the institution of marriage as such. So much hatred breeds within this pious, religious and social bond. It is almost hell to be continuously on war with your own mate, to continuously humiliate and be humiliated in turn. Ila, for all her softness and sophistication, does not spare her husband after her revelation about his promiscuity. Before everyone, she remarks, 'Do you know? Nick's had another of his ideas? He's trying to get my father to buy him a partnership in a warehousing business.

She gave him a long look, her face going hard in a way I had never before noticed in her ' Nick's face crumpled, and he looked down at the carpet, hanging his head' (189). The future lies for Ila, bitter, hard and very painful. But then, there is no one else to blame for it except she, herself. It is pathetic to watch her making up excuses to the narrator about her marriage. She says that whatever she said was wrong and that Nick and she are as happy as ever and the narrator replies, 'of course I believe you, I said. Why shouldn't I? I hope you have a nice time' (248). The tragedy of it tears you apart. Three lives are utterly wasted due to irony of fate.

Irony of fate works in matters of love. Love is a major source of pain in this novel. The state of being in love, the actual mental state of love is a very elusive subject. Love, as it is depicted in popular movies, T.V. serials and popular fiction is not convincing. It is a stereotype that is being repeated a thousand times over. Love is an overplayed and yet not at all understood emotion. To begin with, love is an emotion that centres around one single individual. Now that individual can be anyone—mother, father, beloved, and brother, just anyone. So the very first popular belief that love is only for a suitable mating partner of the opposite sex is wrong. The emotion as such is very wide in its scope. Secondly, love denotes suspension of logic. Love and logic are natural enemies. It also implies that love and every type of rationality *i.e.*, justice, equality etc. are antagonistical. Thirdly, by being irrational, love implies an uncertain, excited and confused state of mind. When one individual becomes the focal point of one's existence, everything and everyone else becomes secondary. Sensible prioritizing in life's agenda is not possible. There is lack of control over emotional life. If we go by the above short description of the emotion of love, we can safely state that the narrator is in love with Tridib, Tha'mma and above everyone with Ila, his silly, beautiful cousin. And I wish to make a sweeping remark here that with none of them he gets his due, just reciprocity. Tridib reciprocates his unconditional hero-worship but only to an extent. Soon May comes and takes the all important eloquence and centrality in his life. The narrator is left high and dry. 'I was jealous, achingly jealous, as only a child can be, because it had always been my unique privilege to understand Tridib, and that day at the Victoria Memorial I knew I had lost that privilege; somehow May had stolen it from me' (170).

With Tha'mma, the pattern takes a different course. As a child, he is soothingly wrapped in her warm protective presence. He gets hysterical once when Tha'mma is hurt. Tha'mma is the narrator's eternal maternal figure with whom he wants to be united. But as he grows, Tha'mma's rules, her unchangeable standards threaten the narrator's identity. He does not want to be engulfed by her. His visits to cheap houses can be taken as his rebellious efforts to free himself from Tha'mma. The narrator goes back to Delhi when Tha'mma's condition improves a little, he tries to unchain his body as well as mind from her powerful grip, 'I jerked my head out of her hands. She met my gaze and smiled. I could not believe that this withered, wasted, powerless woman was the same person that I had so much loved and feared' (91). So, here the umbilical chord between Tha'mma and the narrator breaks.

Finally, with Ila, there never existed any possibility of reciprocity because right from the beginning the scales were so heavily bending to her side. In London many times he walks miles and miles to get to Ila's place, to see her, her laughter, her eyes, to feel her near him but nothing, just nothing comes from her side. The author beautifully explains the connection between love and our tendency to 'enumerate and quantify' (95). We buy heavy physical, material things like jewellery or car to show how much we love. Why does this contradiction exist? Love is the very opposite of these. But the author goes on to explain that just because love is the opposite of justice that we try to apply ordinary rules of wealth and power to normalize it. By applying 'metaphors of normality,' we expect justice in love (96). But it does not happen so. The narrator throws all that he has, his education, appearance, his sweet temperament at Ila's disposal but what he gets, '[...] she would open the door and say Nice to see you, come in, but I hope you're not expecting any dinner—and I would tell her, smiling brightly—I've walked eight miles, it took me exactly two hours and ten minutes—and she would arch her eyebrows in surprise and say: why? Is it some kind of health kick?' (96). So that is what it is. She does not pay any attention to the one who loves her madly and loves the one (Nick) who is not capable of any sincere love. Indeed, there is no logic, no justice in love.

Tha'mma is another pillar of this novel. In her, Ghosh depicts all the peculiarities of a suffering, braving middle class Indian. For all her extremes, she is a real life heroine. She is made of that substance that goes in producing strong, disciplined children and coherent family. Tha'mma became a widow at the age of thirty-two. She joined a school to run her family. She has given her life to her school. She retires from the school as its headmistress. She is sincere, devoted, hardworking, disciplined, all that a teacher is expected to be. She is truly a no-nonsense woman. She cannot see anyone idle in her home. She tells the narrator, her grandson that if anyone wastes time, it starts stinking. She has a militant's attitude to life. She is always on the defensive. There is a very touching incident where Tha'mma does not want any favour even from her own sister, Mayadebi. Mayadebi offers to take them to a place in her car. But Tha'mma does not agree readily to it. The narrator senses 'the fears she had accumulated in the long years after my grandfather's premature death, when she had to take her school teaching job in order to educate my father: I could guess at a little of what it had cost her then to refuse her rich sister's help and of the wealth of pride it had earned her and I knew intuitively that all that had kept her from agreeing at once was her fear of accepting anything anyone that she could not return in exact measure' (33). This is typical middle class mindset. The upper class is used to receiving favours. The lower class cannot refuse them because it needs them badly.

It is only the upright middle class that tries to balance the scales. Tha'mma's whole worldview is around defending herself and her family against a hostile world. We can even call her a feminist in her own way because of her low opinion of men, '[...] at heart she believed that all men would be like him (Tridib) if it were not for their mothers and wives' (6).

Her job becomes her second self. When she gives the narrator a broad, warm smile after her retirement he feels awkward because it was so different from her head mistress's tight-lipped smile. Her involvement in her job is complete. Her farewell at school is very touching. She is full of those small projects, little techniques that a teacher develops in order to improve her/his students. The narrator says, 'when she was headmistress, my grandmother had decided once that every girl who opted for Home Science ought to be taught how to cook at least one dish that was a speciality of some part of the country other than her own. It would be a good way, she thought, of teaching them about the diversity and vastness of the country' (116). Tha'mma's character is a tribute to so many unrecognised women in this country who are holding the world of their children and near and dear ones together by their toil and labour. She brought up her son alone. But she never showed her vulnerability. Her extraordinarily keen observation and the unbending steel of her personality set her in a class of her own. When the narrator is studying at Delhi, Tha'mma gets sick. He comes home to see her. But what does he receive? Tha'mma accuses him of unnecessarily worshipping Ila and also of going to cheep women in Delhi. It is so shocking. The narrator is almost disgusted at the cruelty of her remarks. And when she dies, just a day before, she writes in her firm handwriting to the Principal of the narrator's college that her grandson is visiting cheap houses, that she tried to talk to him but he showed no signs of repentance and that he should be ousted from the college even though he is her own grandson. Can anyone really believe this? The narrator manages to convince the principal of his good conduct and of the sickness that might have affected Tha'mma's mind. After convincing the principal, the narrator writes, 'I have never understood how she learnt of the women I had visited a couple of times, with my friends; nor do I know how she saw that I was in love with Ila so long before I dared to admit it to myself (93). But her character, her behaviour and the consequences of it, like everything else in this book, have a tragic tinge. Basically Tha'mma is a person who has kept her relatives at bay. She never allows relatives to influence her immediate family. Except for her sister, Mayadebi's family, there is hardly anyone who matters to her. But after retirement with 'stinking time,' she derails from her regular path. The family, blood and relatives—these ideas somehow overpower her. The very relatives who have been so hostile, almost enimical, become important to her. The old ghosts come to her that finally claim a precious, young, promising life. But then, life goes on its own course; who can claim to control it. She finds a mission in her old age. The mission is to go back and find about her uncle Jethamoshai and help him if she can. So a lady who 'never pretended to have much family feeling,' suddenly bursts out, 'It doesn't matter whether we recognise each other'or not. We're the same flesh, the same blood, the same bone and now at last, after all these years, perhaps we'll be able to make amends for all that bitterness and hatred' (129). Hardly does she realize that malevolence in human nature does not die. No one, no earthly force can end old bitterness. There is no soap or wash that can clean a heart of its past injuries, humiliation and venom. When she finally gets to meet Jethamoshai, she finds that he has lost his memory. He does not recognise her. But when Tridib reminds him in a loud voice that they are the daughters of his brother who lived in the other part of the house, 'The old man's face lit up. They died! He said, his voice quivering in triumph. They had two daughters: one with a face like a vulture, and another one who was as poisonous as a cobra but all pretty and goody, goody to look at' (214). Just see the irony of it! They have come to rescue him. They are going to lose their child in order to save him and the old man is still spitting venom on them after all those long years. He has not forgotten; he has not forgiven. Old age does not bring nobility with it; it only brings weakness and so perhaps people bend a little due to compulsions. Whatever the truth may be, Tha'mma's visit to Dhaka and her new passion for relatives is the tragic flaw of her personality. And she pays for it. In the end, she has only to say, 'We have to kill them before they kill us' (237).

So, this is the worldly lesson Tha'mma draws from her experiences in life that one has to attack the world before it attacks one. Her defensive posture takes a more rigid form. There are many such ideas that the book suggests. Through trans-border situations Ghosh at times comes with remarkable and relevant ideas regarding civilization, growth and international borders. As the title of the book suggests, all lines are shadow lines; they are not real. Ghosh questions the very basis of modern nation states. It does not matter how many states exist in a continent or sub-continent. It does not change the well being of its people. Nationhood itself is a mirage because it is not based on any logic. When nature draws lines in form of mountains, oceans, rivers, it is real. But man-made borders are shallow and unjustifiable. Jethamoshai speaks well when Tha'mma and others persuade him to go to India, 'Once you start moving you never stop. That's what I told my sons when they took the trains. I said: I don't believe in this India-Shindia. It's all very well, you're going away now, but suppose when you get there they decide to draw another line somewhere? What will you do then? Where will you move? No one will have you anywhere. As for me, I was born here, and I'll die here' (215). In fact, being rooted at a place is a constant thought with Ghosh. It is through Tha'mma that he conveys the idea of self and belonging. When Tha'mma listens to Ila's sad experience at school, when she is not taken care of, by Nick, she only blames Maya and others for living in an alien land, 'it was bound to happen: anyone can see that she has no right to be there. She doesn't belong there.' The message is that one should live with respect where one belongs. Tha'mma believes that those who go and settle abroad do so for money, just for money, nothing else. But with people like Ila, it is perhaps different. Ila wants to live life on the edge. She wants to live dangerously, doing things unconventionally. She tells the narrator that she wants to be part of great events. In her eyes the small events of a backward country like India have no relevance whatsoever. The depthlessness of the present culture is something the author cannot ignore. When the narrator, Ila and Robi go to a nightclub in Calcutta, Ila exerts her freedom. She goes to two businessmen and starts flirting with them. Robi is a physically strong boy. He simply throws away one of the two businessmen. The singing and dancing stops and our trio move out. Ila is humiliated. She shouts, 'Do you see now why I've chosen to live in London? Do you see? It's only because I want to be free.

Free of what? I said.

Free of you! She shouted back. Free, of your bloody culture and free of all of you' (88-89).

So, this is what modern civilization is all about. To be free of commitments, of relationships, of duties, of everything. Live for one's own self—that seems to be the motto. Certainly these crazy, mad, free generations do not wish to taste the joy of surrender, unconditional love and acceptance. I found great symbolism in the incident where Tha'mma searches her house in Dhaka. 'My grandmother, thrown into a sudden panic, began to protest. This couldn't be it, she cried. It can't be our Lane, for where's Kana-babu's sweet shop? That shop over there is selling hammers and hardware: where's the sweet shop gone?' (206). The sweetness of past is gone when the milk of human kindness flooded hearts; this is the age of hammers with which we butcher fellow human beings in the name of religion, caste or boundaries.

Communal hatred and the mechanics of riots is another important dimension of *The Shadow Lines*. Panic, rumour, fear and hatred are universal components of riots. Riots are the same everywhere. There is a very moving account of riots in Calcutta. We see riots as they come to children. Children, narrator as one of them, are struck with fear. He climbs his school bus and everyone stares at his water bottle. He gets unnerved. Then he comes to know that everyone is advised to drink soda as water supply itself has been poisoned. Strange, loud noises are coming to their classroom when Mrs. Anderson is teaching them. They are deported back to their houses amidst a drama of terror and violence. Experiencing the riot, the narrator says, 'The streets had turned themselves inside out: our city had turned against us' (203).

We can compare this to Robi's mental state that resulted from watching the murder of his own brother, Tridib by frenzied rioteers. He is unable to free himself from memories of that terrible event. It comes to him in ghastly forms in his dreams.

We like this book also because of its treatment of India. There are all sorts of pictures of our country but the author is never on the other side; he is always with India. His compassion for his country, howsoever imperfect, does not leave him. So, may be our narcissistic tendencies make us love this book. Right from the importance of Hindi film songs in our lives to centrality of cricket in Indian psyche to the fascination of Indian men for Western dresses to Indian women's love for jewellery—everything is so lovelingly wrapped in this book. When the narrator is going through an acute sensation of love for Ila, he is haunted by an old Hindi film song—'bequraar karke hame yun no jaiyen' (94). He is simply unable to free himself from this recurring tune in his mind. The reader at once identifies with the narrator because with most of the Indians, humming popular film songs to suit their mental condition is a very natural and spontaneous way of purgating emotions. Similarly one is amused to see the narrator's desire to see Ila in Western outfits. When she comes like a true Bengali in a white sari with red border, he is disappointed because it makes her an ordinary next-door girl. Again and again the narrator comments on Ila and her flamboyant Western dresses, 'She was wearing clothes like the one of which I had never seen before, English clothes [...]' (43). Again, 'she looked improbably exotic to me, dressed in a faded blue jeans and a T shirt like no girl I had ever seen before except in pictures in American magazines' (81). It is a regular fantasy of most Indian men to get a Westernized, modern, jeans clad girl and the author so correctly points it here. I cannot help mentioning here the author's portrayal of the exclusive male pleasure of watching girls and women and their spontaneously feminine movements and curves. Our culture perhaps does not condition our women to get the sensuous joy of watching boys and men. It is purely a male domain—'birds watching' as it is popularly known. All these cultural connotations came to my mind reading the narrator's account of watching Ila, 'she was walking slowly, looking down at the pavement, preoccupied, oblivious of the people who stopped to stare at her. I pushed myself back against the pillar, willing her not to see me; I wanted to watch her walking, unselfconscious, for as long as possible' (180).

Similarly, we get valuable information regarding women in India and also women in general. For example, the narrator's mother is fascinated by Shaheb's high-ranking job and his power. He is in foreign services. His photos come in newspapers. When Shaheb makes a polite conversation with her, 'my mother was touched that so important and distinguished a man should take so keen an interest in such trivial and unlikely matters [...]' (40-41). While Shaheb is only making use of his long learned charming social skills, his mother is fascinated. Women are naturally attracted by power. They unconsciously want to conquer the world through the power of the male, their male. This can again be traced back to our culture where outward success and worldly power is associated with men and domestic domain is given to women. So women have no option but to dream of success through men. But domestic domain often creates women with extraordinary worldliness and even cunningness. One cannot help in agreeing with the narrator when he says that housewives accumulate 'manipulative worldliness' (169). And it increases when they are distanced from outside world. We can take the analysis a little further by adding that this manipulative worldliness is the only tool these women have for survival. They have to control their husbands, sons and grandsons in order to secure and maintain their place in the family. Howsoever contradictory it may sound but exposure to the world actually allows space for innocence in a woman's psyche. She can be herself. But if she is grinded in the chores and routine works of domestic existence, she is bound to develop her cunning mechanisms.

But it is not that the author is blind to the grace and joy that an Indian housewife brings to her family. Any man with a working wife can be jealous of the kind of attention and care that the narrator's mother showers on his father. His father is getting rewards of living by convention. His mother eagerly waits for his father to return from office. Transistor and other noises are shunned off. In this serene, wifely atmosphere, she brings 'a clean, fresh kurta and a pair of pyjamas and gently nudge(s) him into the bathroom' (128). And then like a king he sits in an easy chair and she narrates soothingly the events of the day. What a perfect picture!

Now we can think of concluding this discussion on *The Shadow Lines*. The two parts of the book are named (i) *Going Away and* (ii) *Coming Home*. These names are very significant. In fact, coming and going, arriving and leaving, meeting and parting—all metaphors of movement are very important with Amitav Ghosh. His vision seems to hover around these two polarities—coming and going. *Going Away* section comes to an end with Ila's marriage and her going on honeymoon. *Coming Home* section begins with Tha'mma's retirement, farewell, her coming home and ends in the narrator and May lying arms in arms having unfolded the whole truth of Tridib's death. Going Away to me symbolises the author's going away from his real self. Ila is a mirage. His futile chase to get her is nothing but his drifting apart from his self. It symbolises deviation from self. *Coming Home*, it naturally follows, is the narrator's coming to terms with his self and life. It is a journey back home; not running away from roots. After Tha'mma's retirement come the family roots business and her Dhaka trip. One cannot go on living just like that. One has to sort out one's past for one self. And family is part of one's self. Tha'mma and Tridib are part and parcel of the narrator's self. Therefore he comes home with his understanding of Tridib's death. We must remember that the narrator has no name. He has no personality, no identity, and no mark of his own. It is his childhood desire to be Tridib, to be in Tridib's shoes. And that is exactly what he does at the end of the novel, '[...] when we (he and May) lay in each other's arms quietly [...]' (252).

REFERENCE

Ghosh, Amitav. 1988. *The Shadow Lines*. New Delhi: Ravi Dayal Publisher.

4

In an Antique Land

In an Antique Land is essentially a book by an anthropological historian. With serious concerns of a historian, Amitav Ghosh points out at the tragic turn of events in history of Asia and Middle East and particularly India. This book underlines the unarmed nature of Indian trade and commerce before the advent of Vasco-de-Gama in India. The author wants to bring to focus a forgotten period of history, which shows how free and liberal India's collaboration with the Arab, and Chinese world was. He highlights the easy flow of human warmth and trust that existed between a Tunisian Jewish merchant and his Indian helper Bomma. The book is obviously a testimony to Ghosh's intense urge as a tireless, genuine researcher. In fact this book covers Ghosh's research as a social anthropologist over decades. It establishes Ghosh not just as a writer of fiction but also a keen traveller, an diligent researcher, a social anthropologist and a social historian.

At one level, it is a contemporary novel, delineating some ordinary characters. The daily encounters of these characters are shown. Their religious rites, social customs along with their eccentricities and whims are effectively portrayed. A tale grows into a story; ordinariness becomes history; and anthropology mixes with fiction. As someone has remarked that this novel is a change in the ecology of learning.

It is a book first of its own kind by an Indian English writer. In an environment of magical realism, Ghosh's *In an Antique Land* is like a breath of fresh air. Like his other works, his sense of time is not very strict. Time floats and mixes along with blending of fact and fiction, there is coalescing of different branches of knowledge—history, anthropology, philosophy, sociology and religion. It is an interaction of the author with at least four languages and cultures spread across continents and centuries. One thing is certain about Amitav Ghosh—he is not a conventional writer. He is not predictable. He is not the one to produce one novel after another where basic patterns never change and themes keep repeating. As Ghosh has commented on this book in an interview, 'No, this time I'm not writing a novel. Not even sociology, history or belles-letters based on historical research. My new book cannot be described as any one of these. It's a strange sort of a work. Within the parameters of history, I've tried to capture a story, a narrative, without attempting to write a historical novel. You may say, as a writer, I have ventured on a technical innovation' (Net).

The novel is divided in six parts—Prologue, Lataifa, Nashawy, Mangalore, Going Back and Epilogue. It all began in 1942 when Ghosh read an article by E. Strauss. The slave of MSH.6 was referred here by a merchant named Khalaf ibn Ishaq in Aden who in turn got the information by his friend Abraham Ben Yiju in Mangalore, India. Ghosh was hooked by the simple idea that any history of a slave to have survived all these centuries is nothing short of a miracle. When all history is about kings, queens, their carpets, bathtubs, court, courtiers, wars, foreign policy and so on, to find a slave is indeed a wonder. Ghosh did not let go the opportunity and the novel opens, 'The slave of MSH.6 first stepped upon the stage of modern history in 1942' (13).

The second appearance of the slave is in a letter included in a collection by Prof. S.D. Goitein, *Letters of Medieval Jewish Traders*. Ghosh came across this letter in the Bodleain Library at Oxford in the winter of 1978. As a student of social anthropology, Ghosh was leafing through manuscripts. He read about the very same Tunisian Jewish merchant Abraham Ben Yiju who came to India via Egypt around 1130 A.D. Ben Yiju had a slave Bomma who was from Tulunad in India. Ghosh writes, 'I was a student, twenty two years old, and I had recently won a scholarship awarded by a foundation established by a family of expatriate Indians. It was only a few months since I had left India and so I was perhaps a little more befuddled by my situation than students usually are. At that moment the only thing I knew about my future was that I was expected to do research leading towards a doctorate in Social Anthropology. I had never heard of Cairo Geniza before that day, but within a few months I was in Tunisia learning Arabic. At about the same time the next year, 1980, I was in Egypt, installed in a village called Lataifa, a couple of hours journey to the southeast of Alexandria.

I knew nothing then about the slave of MSH.6 except that he had given me a right to be there, a sense of entitlement' (19).

The above lines from the prologue of the novel build a sweet picture of a young, zealous and sincere researcher, emotionally attached to the subject of his research. The names of the next three sections are names of places where the writer went Lataifa, Nashawy and Mangalore. Clearly the picaresque style of Amitav Ghosh continues. In the episodic structure of the book, the author himself is the protagonist and is referred as 'Ya Amitab' by others.

The novel is journey based. Two Indians visit Egypt and Abraham Ben Yiju vigits India. He comes via Egypt and Aden. He lives in India for seventeen long years. His constant companion is a fisherman, Bomma. Bomma is South-Indian. This South-Indian goes to Egypt on business trips on numerous occasions as Yiju's representative. The second Indian to visit Egypt is Ghosh himself. So, as we can see, these two journeys by two Indians to Egypt are separated by centuries. It takes more than a decade for Ghosh to find out all about this relationship between Yiju and Bomma, their respective backgrounds, and personalities. This ground also makes for an interface between Egyptian and Indian civilizations. Ghosh, a thorough social anthropologist catches the storehouse of old records in Babylon. It is the synagogue of Benzra. This is perhaps the biggest single collection of medieval documents ever discovered. They were, however, later taken out of Egypt to Cambridge, Princeton, Oxford and Leningrad. Ghosh assiduously locates Yiju's documents and is first struck by the unusual hybridity of language. The language is Judseo-Arabic, a colloquial dialect of medieval Arabic written in Hebrew script. Ghosh's learning of Arabic proves valuable here. He deciphers all documents and unravels as also rebuilds the story of Ben Yiju and his slave Bomma. We also have inviting description of places like Cairo, Lataifa, Nashawy, Malabar Coast and Mangalore. It is only because of Ghosh's keen knowledge of facts and figures that these descriptions come as true and weighty. There is compactness in Ghosh's words.

Ben Yiju's life is reconstructed with the help of letters between him and his three business partners—Madmun ibn-al-Hasen-ibn-Badar, Yusuf ibn Abraham and Khalaf ibn Ishaq. Ishaq seems to be Yiju's closest friend. Ben Yiju came to Mangalore in 1132 A.D. He married a slave girl Ashu. She is a Nair by caste. Indeed the search for the slave MSH.6 becomes interesting. Moreover it also shows Yiju's total involvement with India. By accepting Ashu in marriage, he shows his flowing sense of humanism. As the three characters in the slave's name are B-M-A, Prof. Goitein suggests the name to be Bama, as derived from Brahma, the creator of the cosmos. But things do not get convincing for Ghosh unless Prof. Vivek Rai of Mangalore University explains things to Ghosh. He tells that the correct name of the slave is Bomma. He was born in a matrilineal community of Tulunad, who worship spirit deities, 'Bhutas.' As we all know, the culture of accepting extra-human and extrasensory phenomena is not new to Indians. This background of Bomma is seems quite natural. The point to be noted, however, is that though Bomma is a mere slave with a meager salary of two dinars per month, he is entrusted with goods worth thousand times more. He is sent as a representative of his master to places like Egypt and Aden. He is a slave and yet not quite a slave. The bond between Yiju and Bomma speaks for the kind of relationship they had. There is trust and commitment in their relationship. Yiju is more like a patron and Bomma like client. There is not much hierarchy. Although Bomma drinks at times, yet his role as Yiju's business agent grows over the years. Yiju has even referred to Bomma as Sheikh in some of his later years marking clearly Bomma's professional rise.

Ghosh suggests that Hinduism has now been standardized and codified. But it was not so always. Bomma belongs to a culture whose popular traditions and folk beliefs 'upturn and invert' categorisation of Sanskritaized Brahiminical Hinduism. This homogenising of our religion where the whole community is expected to be under one umbrella is indeed a new and alien phenomena. It is not in tune with our original religion. This singularity of identity did not exist earlier. Similarly Ben Yiju also followed practices that are now not part of the standard image of the orthodox religions of the Middle East. The popular image of Middle-East religion is quite subversive. But Yiju shares with Bomma the exorcism cults, the magical rites and the custom of visiting graves of different saints. They have a solid meeting ground between them. But for these liberal attitudes 'the matrilinally descended Tulu and the patriarchal Jew would otherwise seem to stand on different sides of an unbridgeable chasm' (263). It is interesting to note how business was conducted in those days between India and Middle East. It was 'wholly indifferent to many of the boundaries that are today thought to mark social, religious and geographical divisions' (278). For example, one of Yiju's business partner Madmun had joint ventures with a Muslim, a Gujrati Bania and a member of a land owning caste of Tulunad. Despite religious, cultural and linguistic differences, they had complete mutual trust and understanding. Perhaps the fact that no legal redress was available in those days enhanced their co-operation. On the front of language Yiju and his associates use a language of Northern derivation. They do not know Tulu. Ghosh goes on to speculate that Yiju and other traders used code words of business. The idea of a specialized trade language reminds us of 'Satti' (wholesale cloth market) of Varanasi where business language is highly specialized. Only years of training yields mastery in this language and its use. But such meaningful and fruitful relationships existed between people of such different backgrounds is stunning indeed. They were making money. They were sharing cultures and religions. They were easily marrying into each other's community. It sounds an utopia even today. But as all good things come to an end, this open, unarmed character of Indian trade was to change forever on 17th May 1498 when Vasco-de-Gama landed in India, 'Within a few years of that day the knell had been struck for the world that had brought Bomma, Ben Yiju, and Ashu together and another age had begun in which the crossing of their paths would seem so unlikely that its very possibility would all but disappear from human memory' (286).

When the Portuguese used military force to capture trade over Indian Ocean and monopolize it, a new era in history as well as thinking began. Ghosh is hardly able to control his anger over colonization, 'Soon, the remains of the civilization that had brought Ben Yiju to Mangalore were devoured by that unquenchable, demonic thirst that had raged ever since, for almost five hundred years, over the Indian ocean, the Arabian Sea and the Persian Gulf (288).

The bulk of the novel constitutes the three visits of Ghosh to Egypt. Ghosh seems enthralled by Egypt and its history. He views the scenario with an exceptional intelligence. His perception is unbiased. He sees people and their lives exactly as they are. However he does not get the same treatment from foreigners. Their treatment of Ghosh is based on the Western view of India. He is even provoked to the extreme. People expect him to fall on his knees whenever a cow passes by. This sort of pinning down attitudes upset him. But among those very foreigners there are individuals like Nabeel who understand his agitation and lovingly reproach him, 'They were only asking questions just like you do; they did not mean any harm. Why do you let this task of cows and burning and circumcision worry you so much? These are just customs; its natural that people should be curious. These are not things to be upset about' (204). But even amidst such sane voices there is confrontation between the two civilizations. All supposedly educatedness comes off and the mask of civilization is broken when Ghosh fiercely defends his country' against the brutal attack of Imam. However the impact of this incident on Ghosh is shattering. It was the death of a dream that he saw in history, 'I was crushed, as I walked away; it seemed to me that the Imam and I had participated in our own final defeat, in the dissolution of the centuries of dialogues that has linked us [...] we had acknowledged it was no longer possible to speak as Ben Yiju or his slave, or as one of the thousands of travellers who had crossed the Indian Ocean in the Middle Ages might have done; of things that were right or good, or willed by God' (236-37). Ghosh even feels guilty that he has betrayed the period of history that he is studying. He is sorry that he is not able to keep up the spirit of Ben Yiju and Bomma.

The book also makes a comment on the growing trend of consumerism and its impact on the developing world. When Ghosh returns to Egypt after seven years he finds major changes in the two villages. The young men of these villages have gone to Gulf countries and have brought huge sums of money. When Ghosh visits Abu-Ali in Lataifa with Seikh Musa, he witnesses a procession of, 'A T.V. set, a food processor, a handful of calculators, a transistor radio, a couple of cassette players, a pen that was also a flash light, a watch that would play tunes, a key ring that answered to a hand clap and several other such objects' (Ghosh: 293). When he goes to the house of Abu Ali, he finds that it has vanished. Instead of the old dilapidated house, a brightly painted three storeyed building stands. Instead of the old moped there is now a new pick-up Toyota truck. Ghosh is, 'assaulted by a sudden sense of dislocation,' as though he had gone to different epochs. The magic of immigrant labour has changed the world of Lataifa and Nashawy beyond reorganization in less than a decade. What has changed is not merely the physicality of things but the inner socio-cultural relationships have also been, 'upturned and rearranged.' It does not need much imagination to see that Ghosh is not only talking about the villages of Egypt only but is referring to the paradigmatic changes occurring in all developing countries like his own. Herein lies the contemporary relevance of the book.

The idea that all divisions are unreal and artificial appears again and again in Ghosh's fiction. At the end of his second visit to Egypt, before leaving for Cairo Ghosh wishes to visit the tomb of a saint called Sidi-Abu-Hasira but he is taken by the police and is interrogated by the chief. The police officer is simply unable to understand why an Indian who is not Jewish wants to visit the tomb of a Jewish holy man. This is again a significant remark on the current culture of intolerance. In this case religion is causing walls. Ghosh is unable to stop himself from telling the police officer the story of Ben-Yiju and Bomma. He tells him that these two gentlemen of past shared 'indistinguishable intertwined histories, Indian and Egyptian, Muslim and Jewish, Hindu and Muslim' (339). But the police officer is not ready to understand. He again goes back to dissuading Ghosh from visiting the saint's tomb. He says that all these superstitious beliefs will disappear with development and progress. Ghosh leaves the scene saying that this is indeed a heavy price for development and progress.

The novel ends with his last visit to Egypt in 1990, just three weeks after the Iraqi invasion of Kuwait. There is a sense of disappointment at the protracted Iran-Iraq war. In all these scenes, human concerns go unabated. Nabeel hopes that things will return to normal and soon he will be able to earn enough money for the ongoing renovation of his house.

REFERENCE

Ghosh, Amitav. 1992. *In An Antique Land*. New Delhi: Ravi Dayal Publisher.

5
The Calcutta Chromosome

The Calcutta Chromosome, like almost all other works of Amitav Ghosh, is an experimental work. Except *The Shadow Lines* and *The Glass Palace* none of what Ghosh has done clearly qualifies as fiction or history, fantasy or thriller. It is such an amalgamated body of work. It is so confusing, so alluring, and so gripping. *The Calcutta Chromosome* is a lovely piece of work. It has science, religion, myth, nihilism, transcendental philosophy, Indian superstitions, logic, rationality and what not. In the boiling cauldron of his brain, Ghosh has cooked a mixed dish for us. But it is certainly tasty. For the commentator, however, the problem remains—where to begin, where to end. The best approach would be to begin straight away—express the ideas as they come. This book evokes responses. So, let me fast record my responses to *The Calcutta Chromosome*.

Ghosh digs into one event, one pinpointed happening of the past. He keeps probing it till he finds patterns, and parallels. It is wonderful to watch this artist work. He selects an event that he feels is relevant to present times. He establishes connections. He says what he wants to say using symbols of past only as tools for the communication of his overall message or messages. On the face of it, this book is about malaria. It is an attempt to rewrite the story of Ronald Ross's discovery of the life cycle of malaria mosquito and how it causes the disease to human beings. As such, this story is very much available in the annals of medical history. Ross is not new to Indians. Almost every student of Indian schools has gone through a lesson on Ronald Ross, his discovery and his winning the Nobel Prize for it. This British bacteriologist is more close to people of Calcutta as he did his path breaking research in this city only. His memorial arch at the entrance of the P.G. Hospital is part and parcel of Calcutta. The fact that despite the sensational research, the disease still goes unabated, taking its annual toll of human lives, generates regret. We feel, 'It's not so great after all.' From generating this sense initially, Ghosh begins his work of undoing the aura around Ross. He seems to say, 'Okay, he found out anopheles, so what?'

Ross discovered the deadly female mosquito on 20th August 1897. Except for this fact, Ghosh has totally deviated from the known accounts of this event. It is his own story. He has divided the book into two parts, (i) August, 20: Mosquito Day and (ii) The Day After. L. Murugan is a science freak. He is obsessed with the idea of finding all the facts (known or less known) about the malaria story. On World Mosquito Day 20th Aug., 1995, he arrives in Calcutta. He is in search of the enigmatic Calcutta Chromosome. This Calcutta Chromosome, as we shall see later in detail, is a freak chromosome. It is unusual because it cannot be isolated and detected by standard techniques. Unlike our regular chromosomes, it is not present in every cell. It is not even symmetrically paired. It does not run from one generation to the other. Ghosh fantasise that this chromosome develops out of a process of recombination, which is unique to every individual. It is found only in the non-regenerating tissue, the brain. It can be transmitted through malaria. It is this stray DNA carrier that Murugan calls 'The Calcutta Chromosome'—a unique 'biological expression of human tracts that is neither inherited from the immediate gene-pool, nor transmitted into it' (207).

But as Murugan arrives at Calcutta, the very next day he mysteriously disappears. At the heart of the narrative lie the events of these days. All other strands of narrative are connected to this main event. The medical history of malaria, Ross's progress in his research, experiences of Antar, Murugan's former colleague at New York and some scattered incidents at Calcutta are woven into a fictional fabric.

The major part of the story takes place in Calcutta in 1995. The novel follows Murugan and his adventures closely. The laboratory of the P.G. Hospital of Calcutta is the place where Ronald Ross made the final breakthrough in his research. The fact that Ross discovered the cause of malaria in Calcutta, (India) has deeper connotations for those who are conscious of colonization. In the whole world it was India with all its filth, garbage, and puddles that nurtured sufficient number of mosquitoes to make the research possible. Since mosquito cannot be taken as a symbol for cleanliness, the place where it resides is naturally dirty. Ghosh, in fact, uncovers the whole power politics of the West. This book is an attempt to deconstruct Western aura. It shows that the Western sense of confidence and patronage is misplaced. It is a false notion that it guides the destiny of the post colonial nations. The narrative covers over a hundred years. The cinematic devices of flash forward or flashback come handy to Ghosh. As is clear, he mingles fact with fiction unobtrusively. At one level the reader is willingly taken on a journey into time and at the same time to different countries like America, England, Egypt and India. Ghosh compresses or expands according to his convenience the actual time period of an event. This highlights the parallels between two events that took place at two different periods of time. This technique also constructs contrasts between two events of different periods. Apart from this we can visually cement the gap between seemingly distant actions.

The most unique feature operating in the text of the novel is its questioning of the past. Our historical fixities are questioned. Ghosh is obviously skeptical towards the towering altitude given to a certain period or event. Murugan is the voice of rationality. He senses certain discrepancies in Ronald Ross's account of 'Plasmodium B.' Murugan is unable to free himself from the idea of something being foul in the medical history of malaria. He is preparing an article, 'An Alternative Interpretation of Late 19th Century Malaria Research. Is There A Secret History?' Long back when Murugan was in New York he had written a summary of his research in an article entitled, 'Certain Systematic Discrepancies in Ronald Ross's Account of Plasmodium B.' To his shock Murugan received a very hostile' response from the scientific community. All scientific journals rejected the paper. The fact that he doubted Ross's greatness costs him the membership of Science Society. He was called a crank and an eccentric. Naturally all this did not help Murugan. He became more and more obsessed and erratic. He began to publicize his ideas about the other mind behind Ross's discovery. His theory is that some persons systematically interfered with Ross's experiment and pushed Malaria research into the right direction. He believes that Ronald Ross who was awarded the Noble Prize in 1906 for his work on the life cycle of the Malaria vector had been handed the information on a plate. It was not his discovery at all. Someone else had planted the idea in his head that Malaria parasite could be found in one of the species of mosquitoes. Murugan is convinced that a big conspiracy was played in 1895. Originally Ross was on a completely wrong track. Even Ross's mentor Patrick Manson, the noted Scottish bacteriologist who had written a book on Filaria was on a wrong track. Both Manson and Ross thought that Malaria parasite was transmitted from mosquitoes to human beings orally, probably through drinking water. But almost overnight Ross changed his track and on August 20th, 1897 he found the connection between Plasmodium Zygotes and Anopheles, Stephensil. Murugan finds it hard to swallow that Ross could be successful in such a short span of time. Keeping the complexities of the research in mind it ought to have taken longer period of time. His curiosity and rationality force him to pursue his search of what actually happened and how it happened. Ghosh goes on to suggest that Ronald Ross had two assistants, Mangala a sweeper woman and Laakhan (Lutchman), who is a 'Dhooley-bearer.'

But before going deeper let us first decipher three different levels of the narrative. In one strand of the story-line we have Antar, an Egyptian computer clerk. Antar works day and night all alone on his super intelligent computer named Ava. He is working in the early part of the 21st century. He tries to relocate the adventures of an India born American scientist L. Murugan. Antar tries to find out the reason behind the incomprehensible fact that Murugan disappeared in Calcutta in 1995. The second level of the story-line is historically true and it revolves around the British Scientist Ronald Ross, who discovered the manner in which malaria is conveyed by the mosquito in 1902. The third level describes the super human powers of Mangala and Laakhan. At this level Ross's result is reduced to a subordinate activity only which, is controlled by more potent power of Mangala and Laakhan. The story begins in a New York apartment where Antar is working. In fact Antar works for the International Water Council, a global organisation that explores and examines the depletion of the world's water supplies. One morning the computer Ava jerkingly produces an I.D. Card with a small mettle chain attached to it. The card is badly damaged, symbolizing for us the bruised ego of the card owner. When Antar gives the necessary commands Ava with its astounding resourcefulness, recreates the card. It becomes clear that the card had originated in Calcutta. It also creates a holographic projection of the man to whom the card once belonged. Antar comes to know that the man was L. Murugan, who had worked for a non-profit organisation that served as a global public health consultancy and epidemiological data bank. Actually Antar had also worked there once. Murugan has thin and discoloured hairs. His eyes are bright black. He has a moon like face. His nose is that of a boxer, and he has an aggressively jutting chin. Overall Murugan makes for a combative, obstinate and unstoppable man. Murugan happens to be the most entertaining character of the novel as well. He claims to be the only expert on the Ronald Ross in the world. The great love of his life is uncovering the medical history of malaria. We can easily see that Ghosh wants to give recognition to the less known, less fortunate people. The world worships success. Many times the deserving go unnoticed. Murugan's only crime is that he has dared to disagree. He doubts the set beliefs.

Murugan gets convinced that there was a conspiracy behind malaria research. He leaves for Calcutta in search of all missing links, which could enlighten him and the world about the century old puzzle. His friends and wellwishers try to dissuade him but Murugan is determined. He reaches Calcutta on 20th August 1995 and the very next day vanishes. With use of cinematic techniques, on one hand, Ross is shown making the final breakthrough and on the other hand Murugan is trying to prove his hypothesis that Ross had been literally led by the nose to the discovery by forces beyond his comprehension. The fuelling agencies of the novel are Antar's curiosity and Murugan's skepticism. Howsoever imaginative it may sound, Ghosh seems to believe in marginality or alternative reality. In Calcutta Murugan spots all the missing links as well as the conspirators. The conspirators are the well-established people of the society-writers, journalists, film stars and businessmen. Smoothly floating through past, present and future Murugan weaves the narrative into a coherent whole. The conspiracy seems to be eternal. It is the conspiracy of a mediocre society against those who are deserving, original and genuine. The conspirators try to confuse Murugan and trap him into their experiment. By the end of the story even Antar is dragged into their fold. This team of people has its own aims. They desire a journey to the unknown. Their quest is for immortality. Ghosh believes that the purpose of science is not only to reveal but also to create. Awareness is the key. Whatever is known is knowledge. At the other end of the scientific knowledge lies the unknown, unarticulated truth. That truth may be unknown but the point is that it is very much there. Keeping all the mess in scientific research in mind, Ghosh creates a group of bright researchers whose ultimate aim is to keep their research a secret. They try to conceal their inventions. The source of their strength is silence.

Phulboni is the greatest living writer of Bengal. He has also won the national award. He is the chief exponent of this cult of silence. This team consists of marginalised people. Some of these people were picked up by Dr. D.D. Cunningham from the railway station to serve him as research assistants. Incidentally it was at Cunningham's laboratory only Ross discovered the Malaria bug. Ghosh seems to have taken the beliefs of these people directly from Derrida. Their idea is that 'knowledge is self contradictory [...] they believed that to know something is to change it, therefore in knowing something, you have already changed what you think you know so you don't really know it at all. You only know its history [...] they thought that knowledge couldn't begin without acknowledging the impossibility of knowledge I...] if it's true that to know something is to change it, then it follows that one way of changing something, of effecting a mutation, [...] is to attempt to know it, or aspects of it' (88).

Thus the fantasy goes on that in counter-science, secrecy is used as a technique of procedure. For this group of bright researchers, silence is the only religion. Ghosh also suggests that an Austrian clinician Julius Von Wagner Jauregg was actually ahead of Ronald Ross on malaria research. He was working on the clue that artificially induced malaria could cure or at least mitigate syphilitic paresis. But even before the Austrian in the 1890's Mangala, a sweeper woman had achieved remarkable success in this field. Mangala herself suffered from syphilis whom Dr. Cunningham had found at Sealdah station and trained her as a laboratory assistant. Murugan believes that Mangala was a genius. She had a strong intuition. She was going in the right direction in malaria research due to her instinctive understanding. Murugan also guesses that Mangala was using a variation of Wagner process. She had perhaps noticed that malaria works on paresis through a different route, the brain. Like syphilis, malaria can cause irreparable damage to the brain, it can even cause hallucination. Perhaps that is why primitive people thought of malaria as spirit-possession. India has a very deep and long tradition of the occult. People are highly superstitious. In fact spirits (Bhuta-pret) are considered to be as real as the human beings by the uneducated, rural masses of India. The bhuta-pret are said to exist in a half way house between the human world and the world of ancestral spirits (pitri-lok). Until they have been judged, have paid their 'karmic' debts and are allowed into the world of ancestral spirits, the 'bhuta-pret' continue to yearn for a human body which they can enter and contrive to make sick through their nefarious activity. These spirits, occupying the lowest rungs in the Hindu hierarchy of supernatural beings, are closest to human state. Whatever the reason, both the 'bhuta-pret' and the 'pitri' are a tangible, living presence for most people. They seem to populate a mental region that is contiguous and has open borders with the land of ordinary consciousness in which normal everyday life takes place.

Interestingly Ghosh deconstructs and dismantles Western sense of superiority by Indian irrationality. These beliefs are said to have no scientific basis, yet their strong presence in India can easily be felt. Deconstruction, in the Derridian context is a nihilistic activity. And yet to perform this nihilistic activity Ghosh uses the tool of blind religious beliefs. This is indeed an interesting contradiction of this book.

Mangala had developed a particular kind of malaria that could be induced in pigeons. Here we may remember that Mangla is the other name of the great mother Kali who comes in various forms in Indian mythology. She is the archetypal nurturer as well as the terrible mother figure. She is the life giver as well as the annihilator. We may also remember that pigeons are an inseparable part of the famous witchcraft of

Bengal. Even today at Kamakhyan temple in Assam, the highest seat of Indian black magic, pigeons are regularly used in various rituals. Murugan who is unearthing Mangala's story also has a significant name. Murugan is the other name of Kartik, the son of the goddess who is reputed for swift movements in Indian mythology. So approximately speaking, here is a son figure trying to get credit for the mother figure, which she richly deserves. Now Mangala had also developed the technique of transferring malaria from a pigeon to a patient of syphilis. Secretly she started treating patients in Cunningham's laboratory. Her treatment produced strange side effects. The patients often developed weird personality disorders. These symptoms in the patients were actually 'randomly assorted personality traits' which the patient imbibed from the malaria donor *i.e.*, the pigeon. Actually this process hinted at the freak chromosome, which had earlier been described as the unique Calcutta Chromosome. The special contribution that the Calcutta Chromosome makes is that it suggests transference of personality traits. In this way it suggests immortality. As Murugan excitedly tells his researcher Antar. 'Just think, a fresh start: when your body fails you, you leave it, you migrate—you or at lest a matching symptomlogy of yourself. You begin all over again, another body, another beginning [...] a technology that lets you improve on yourself in your next incarnation' (91-92).

Murugan has spent many years on his extensive research. His clues indicate that Ross's discovery was only a small part of the overall project of Mangala to attain immortality through the Calcutta Chromosome. By 1897 Mangala had run into a dead end. She tried again and again to stabilize and catch the chromosome in the process of transmission. But she failed. She needed more information on the malaria bug. That is why she needed Ross's help, 'She actually believed that the link between the bug and the human mind was so close that once its life-cycle had been figured out, it would spontaneously mutate in directions that would take her work to the next step' (208). But to know something is to create it. Breaking the law of silence she planted crucial clues in Ross's head and took the research in the right direction. Ross was just a tool. Murugan also believes that Mangala and Laakhan did succeed in transplantation of the Calcutta Chromosome. In fact Laakhan himself is a living example of interpersonal transference of the Calcutta Chromosome. This malevolent character with a deformed hand is 'all over the map, changing names, switching identities' (74).

Both Laakhan and Mangala are characters who change identities. Ghosh has underlined the value of secrecy in matters of intellectual property. The whole atmosphere of the book suggests that there is much theft and deceit in this field. There is one Elijah Monroe who comes to Cunningham's Laboratory to detect the ongoing experiments. Laakhan stages a train accident and finishes Elijah Monroe. Similarly another friend of Ross J.W.D. Grigson also faces a near fatal accident in Secundarabad when he senses that something crucial is going on. Laakhan also meets Phulboni thirty-six years after Grigson episode. It clearly means that it is not exactly Laakhan who meets Phulboni but his spirit or his spirit in some other body. Phulboni is writing a set of stories on Laakhan. The real name of Phulboni is Saiyad Murad Hussain. He is an eminent writer. He has taken the tribal name, Phulboni. This character is designed to convey the author's viewpoint from time to time. The two names are there to emphasize the confusion and duality of self. Everyone is like that. The mythological references of names at times make the characters archetypes. Mangala, the sweeper woman also appears in different forms. When Murugan comes to Calcutta in 1995 to find about the malaria story, he discovers an esoteric cult of image worshippers. Murugan comes to know that the image is that of Mangala. She is called 'Mangalabibi.' People worship to commemorate her reincarnation. Phulboni does a comprehensive story on this image and its advent into the world. Through this Goddess metaphor, Ghosh insists on the necessity of coming back to life. No one dies. Nothing ends. Resurrection is a must. The journey of the soul independent of any particular body is an established Hindu concept. The body dies but the soul travels into another body and lives on. Soul is imperishable. The movement of soul from one body to another and its final merger with the super soul is controlled by God. God is the supreme power. But Mangala, a human being, attempts to master the art of transferring souls. She wants to be the controlling consciousness, the mind that sets things in motion. It hardly needs an explanation now that Mangala also symbolises the ultimate desire of a human being to become God. In polite terms, it can be described as the wish of a human being to merge in the womb of the supreme mother. As we know in 'Bhakti marg' where poet/devotee/mystic cries in anguish to become one with mother. Mangala belongs to this path. The other path is that of 'Tarka' or logic and science. Ross follows this path. The two paths may seem contradictory but in reality are not so. They are complementary. In fact, in this book, Ghosh ratifies and endorses Mangala's path. Logic? without intuition is incomplete. Ross's research has been attributed a secondary place while Mangala's methods have been hailed as perfect. As has been pointed out earlier, Western aura has been undone.

The Indian myth of Ganesh has also been used to explain Indian concept of changing identities. A child with an elephant head is a clear sign of possibility and acceptance of duality of personality. Ghosh with a strong nationalist vein tries to establish Indian supremacy in the world of knowledge and science.

Coming back to Mangala and Laakhan, we cannot ignore the fact that both of them are from the very lowest rung of Hindu caste system. Here is a desired reversal of roles. Mangala of the sweeper caste is worshippal in blood and flesh as well as years after as an image. Farley, a Western scientist watches this scene where Mangala is deified despite her social class,

'[...] the woman Mangala was seated at the far end of the room, on a low divan, but alone and in an attitude of command, as though enthroned. By her side at the far end of the room were several bamboo cages, each containing a pigeon. They were all slumped on the floor of death [...] on the floor by the divan, clustered around the woman's feet, were some half dozen people in various attitudes of supplication, some touching her feet, others lying prostrate. Two or three others were huddled against the wall, wrapped in blankets (...] they were syphilitics, in final stages of the terrible disease' (125-26).

Ghosh seems adamant that the repositories of truth, science and higher knowledge can be a 'dhooley bearer' Laakhan and a sweeper woman Mangala. He demolishes the false concept that class superiority and right to knowledge go together. Here is wishful undoing of Indian caste system and an assertion of the right to knowledge irrespective of class, caste, creed, culture or colour. Twice in the course of the novel, Laakhan is shown as a torch bearer; metaphorically a bearer of knowledge. Ghosh further universalises the theory by making people of all religious background accepting the entire drama. Hindus (Murugan, Sonali, Urmila), Muslims (Saiyad Murad Hussain alias Phulboni, Antar) and Christians (Mrs. Aratounian and Countess Pongracz)—all accept the transmigration of souls.

By bringing the underprivileged to the focus of attention, Ghosh is hinting at the current justified trend in the field of scientific research where the rights of 'subjects' are fervently advocated, especially in the field of social medicine, health, hygiene and control of epidemics. Human or animal subjects who are experimented upon, are perhaps more important than the researcher. We may recall it was Laakhan who offered to drink Ronnie's (Ross's) medicine first. Ghosh tries to bring recognition to those who do the spade work for all the grand discoveries. Another recent trend suggests that health and bioresearch can be conducted more economically and efficiently if local people are given principal place in it. They know their soil better than those sitting in saniticized laboratories and working on fanciful hypothesis.

Ghosh writes about a vanished era. He is interested in past. Yet he is a modern writer because modernity is not about the surface details of a story. It hardly matters into which period the actual fable is cast. What matters is the manner, depth and quality of the author's response. This is exactly what makes Ghosh relevant to us. I see this novel as a statement on the necessary isolation of an individual and the role of introspection and silence in it. We are social beings—true! But we are equally individual beings. The separation of the individual's entity is essential for any creative or genuine work or for life, for that matter. At the heart of existence lies a still point, silence and isolation. And this need not be taken in post-modern sense of alienation, communicationlessness or absurdism. No, not at all. It is what the psychologists call the individuation process where a human being realises that she/ he is separate from others. It is only after this realization that the merger into the whole, the next stage comes. I am reminded of what T.S. Eliot wrote in the first part of Four Quartets, Burnt Norton:

'At the still point of the turning world.
Neither flesh nor fleshless;
Neither from nor towards;
At the still point, there the dance is,
But neither arrest nor movement.
And do not call it fixity,
Where past and Future are gathered.
Neither movement from nor towards;
Neither ascent nor decline.
Except for the point, the still point,...'

This is pure Vedanta. It will not be far-fetched in my opinion to bring this idea directly to this book. Let us have a look at principal characters of this novel. Antar is a widower. His neighbours have a shadow existence for him. Ava, the supercomputer is his only companion. He is connected to other human beings only through his machine. Murugan is a divorcee. He is companionless except for the ghosts from the past. Antar, Urmila, Sonali and Mrs. Aratounian are his acquaintances; but none are his friends. Urmila may have a family theoretically but practically she is an alien. Her vulnerability due to loneliness is obvious. Sonali is an illegitimate child of Phulboni. She is an actress and lives all by herself. Mrs. Aratounian does not seem to have any family or friend. Phulboni is a typical loner, roaming in the streets of Calcutta all by himself. Mangala and Laakhan are above their community. They are revered but are never befriended. They are not treated as close associates. Ronald Ross has a family but only in the background. He is emotionally estranged from all co-creatures. He is deep into the bug. Antar, as we see, is frightened at this drama of isolation at the end of the novel. But as I said, this loneliness is not the loneliness of O'Neill, or Beckett, or Amis, or Miller and the like. Antar is coming from an assembly of people. Suddenly, he is alone. Yet he feels their presence in his New York apartment, '[...] they were saying 'we're with you. You are alone; we'll help you across.' He sat back, and sighed as he hadn't sighed in years' (Ghosh: 256). I take sighing to be a sure sigh of emotions and emotions take us to community and positivism.

But the point is that realisation of individuality is a must. The one who works has an inner life separate from the lives of others. And silence is the only companion here. Language becomes useless, at least insufficient. As Byron said and I vaguely remember, 'There's much company when none speaks.' Let me quote the beautiful words of Ghosh himself, 'Mistaken are those who imagine that silence is without life, that it is inanimate, without either spirit or voice. It is not: indeed the word is to this silence what the shadow is to the foreshadowed what the veil is to the eye, what the mind is to truth, what language is to life' (40).

REFERENCE

Ghosh, Amitav. 1966. *The Calcutta Chromosome*. New Delhi: Ravi Dayal Publisher.

6

Dancing in Cambodia, At Large in Burma

Amitav Ghosh's training as an anthropologist has been an important formative factor in his books. Travelling comes naturally to him. As such much of what he has written is travel based but this book *Dancing in Cambodia, At Large in Burma* is a pure travelogue. With an anthropologist's eye for accuracy and authenticity Amitav Ghosh's studies life, art, culture, and social and political institutions of the places he visits. Thematically speaking, displacement has been a central concern of Ghosh's work. Coming and going, departures and arrivals have always been relevant symbols of his narrative structure. Travel is a very complex psychological process. It changes the traveller in many ways. If travelling is juxtaposed with living at a fixed place, we can easily see the influences of travelling on a person. To begin with it makes a person more flexible in her/his routine and life style. It opens new possibilities in her/ him regarding both the world and her/his own self. The traveller seems to realise, 'I never knew these things existing in the world as well as I never knew I had all these possibilities in me.' Naturally reading about a place is as different from actually visiting it as getting a description of a sweet piece and actually eating it.

Travelling can be either real or fictional or a combination of both. But here we are talking about real travelling. Travelling can be for a definite purpose like earning money or getting education and knowledge. It can be just for fun as well. In the present world many travels are aimed at searching the roots.

At times the traveller may be irresistibly in love with a particular place. There can be a thousand more reasons for travelling. In any case travelling remains a powerful human sensation, a jolt.

V.S. Naipaul and Salman Rushdie have also written travelogues. Naipaul is, of course, the most famous travel writer of our times. But it will need a separate book to discuss his travel writings. Salman Rushdie in the prologue to his travelogue *Jaguar Smile* says that when he visited Nicaragua he never intended to write a book or write at all for that matter. But the Nicaraguan experience shook him so deeply that he had no choice left but to record all his experiences in the form of a travelogue. We can take Ghosh's travelogue in the light of above comment. Only a writer who has a proper sense of time and distance can write a good travelogue. For one thing, travel writing is always nostalgic. The writer here is trying to capture various images of a place or places, she/he has to balance the time of her/his actual visiting and writing and also the distance between her/his place and the place she/he is writing about. But this is not all. The travel writer has to weigh the flow of time and its distance in the place of his/her description. For example in writing about Cambodia and Burma Ghosh has to view these countries in historical perspective. One just cannot grasp the chaotic realities of present day Cambodia and Burma unless one knows how the time has roughly flown in those countries. On matters as sensitive and controversial, as the regime of Pol Pot and the emotionally charged movement of Suu Kyi, the writer must save herself/himself from the dangers of morbidity, glib sensationalism or excessive sermonizing and moralizing. Going by these rules we can say that Ghosh has done a wonderful job. As a perspective author and politically alert observer Amitav Ghosh has tried to comprehend Cambodia and Burma and their respective recent pasts of extreme isolation. Both the countries have been colonized earlier; both had traumatic dictatorial regimes. And both the countries practised politics of complete isolation or iron curtain in recent past. Ghosh tries to reconstruct the scenario during the regime of isolation. The book is a significant social-historical chronicle. It is divided into three parts— (i) Dancing in Cambodia, (ii) Stories in Stone and (iii) At Large in Burma.

It is a small book where the first and third chapters are of about fifty pages each and the middle one is literally sandwiched into eleven pages.

King Sisobath was the last king of Cambodia before Pol Pot took over. The first chapter begins with an anthropological description of the sea journey of King Sisobath. Cambodia as we all know had been colonized by the French. It was king Sisobath's life long dream to visit the land of the colonizers *i.e.*, France. We can see Ghosh's reconstruction of the mind set of the colonized. Sisobath went along with his entourage of several dozen princes, courtiers, officials, and most importantly a troupe of nearly a hundred traditional classical dancers and musicians from his royal palace in Phnom Penh. His journey started on 10th May 1906 in the afternoon. He was abroad a French Liner, Amiral Kersaint. We can only smile at the child like joy of the king and his group, The king, who had been crowned two years before, had often spoken of his desire to visit France, and for him the voyage was the fulfilment of a lifelong dream' (1).

For other members also it was a cherished opportunity to step out of their cloistered existence. They were going to perform for the colonizers. It was their moment of showing and proving themselves at the immense fairyland, Marseille where an exhibition had been organized on the theme of France's colonial possessions. They were going out of their country for the first time. As Ghosh touchingly writes about the royal dancers, 'It was said that the dancers entered the palace as children and spent their lives in seclusion ever afterwards; that their lives revolved entirely around the royal family; that several were the king's mistresses and had even born him children; that some of them had never stepped out of the palace grounds until this trip to France' (3).

The colonized situation of dancers is sensitively portrayed. Their excitement and joy at visiting the 'superior' land on one hand and their inferiority complex and anxiety on the other have been described in a very delicate fashion. There is no doubt that Ghosh is a master in the craft in weaving words. It is almost impossible to change or replace his words. Precision is his supreme attribute. When he describes these dancers there is no sexual undertone as might be expected. There is nothing erotic in his vision. He describes them just as they are. We can almost pity the dancers, '[...] with their hard and close-cropped hair, their fingers like those of striplings, their thin, muscular legs like those of young boys, their arms and hands like those of little girls, they seem to belong to no definite sex. They have something of the child about them, something of the young warrior of antiquity and something of the woman' (4). Accompanying these excited dancers, as their guide and head is king Sisobath's eldest daughter princess Soumphady. An elegant lady with an immense presence, royal manner and style, she has an electrifying effect on the audience at Marseille. We shall see later that her impact on the art and culture of Cambodia has been of a permanent nature. She is her own woman. A woman of substance, we might call her in current terminology. She admires the French women, their clothes and head dresses but nevertheless declines to dress up like them. She holds her ground, 'No! The princess said after a moment's reflection. No! I am not used to them and perhaps would not know how to wear them' (5). This can also be taken as an indirect hint at the Indians' fascination for Western style of dressing. Almost a century back these Cambodian women had a sense of pride about their distinctive attire suited for the variety of their dances.

Conversation with the associates of Pol Pot is a major and effective research device adopted by Ghosh. He learns about the remaining story of the journey to France and other aspects of the Pol Pot regime through Chea-Samy, a sister-in-law of Pol Pot and a teacher at the school of fine arts in Phnom-Penh, in 1993. Chea-Samy is the main agent who tells the author about the tearing apart of Cambodia by tyrannical Pol Pot years from 1975 to 1978 and the incessant turmoil thereafter. Ghosh meets the members of Pol Pot's family. He also visits the village where he was born to gain insight into his background. Ghosh tries to assess the impact of Pol Pot's brutal regime on Cambodia. What is striking is the power of dance and music and the vital force of these arts operating upon the Cambodian collective psyche. Howsoever hard it may be for believing, but it is these art forms that hold Cambodia intact after the traumatic years. In this saga of cultural courage, the importance of dance in Cambodia has been paramount even when the country is on the brink of destitution. The tenacity of Cambodian people is touching.

The Khmer Rouge leader Pol Pot died of heart attack in April 1998 at the age of seventy-two. His real name was Saloth Sar. He grew up in a comparatively prosperous farming family at the hilly area of Kompong Thong province. This area was the very centre of the then French protectorate. He got a scholarship in 1949 and studied Radio Electronics in Paris. His political career began in 1950 when he joined the underground communist party. He became its general secretary in 1962. He finally came to power in 1975. As soon as he came to power, he started implementing his dream of turning Cambodia into an agrarian utopia where there would be no city, no money, no property and no religion. He held all these things to be the corrupting forces. He started setting up rural collectives. He was completely ruthless in his implementation of his vision of a perfect society. Whosoever was even remotely sensed as being 'liberal' or against his views was executed. He was the architect of Cambodia's killing fields. He is held responsible for the deaths of two million Cambodians! It was only in his death in 1998 that international community shook in commotion and tried to inquire about his motives and methods. Since then, many people have tried to know the reasons and aftereffects of Pol Pot's terrible graduation from electronic engineering to social engineering. He was held possessed by the idea of social cleansing. Pol Pot's activities amount to one of the worst genocides in the twentieth century. 'Dancing in Cambodia' is an answer to all questions regarding Pol Pot's regime of isolation.

Chea-Samy had entered the palace in Phnom Penh in 1925 as a child of six. She began her training in classical dance under princess Soumphady's guidance. Ghosh also meets Molyka, a mid-level civil servant. Ten members of Molyka's family had been murdered by Pol Pot, including her father! We can only imagine the depth of torture, sorrow and the mental damage caused by Pol Pot. Pol Pot's ideas of Social Utopia were shaped by his early life among the hill tribes in remote northeastern Cambodia. The tribe was called Khmers. These early Khmers were self-sufficient. They lived a sort of ideal community life or so it must have looked to Pol Pot. Their raw culture was unaffected and untainted by Buddhism. They had no concept of money. It was somehow Pol Pot's umbilical attachment with his childhood that resulted in all that bloodshed and horror. Pol Pot went about his plan in a systematic manner. He targeted the middle class. In his recent book, *The Great Indian Middle Class*, the bureaucrat turned writer Pawan Varma, has dealt in detail about the tenacity and high endurance level of Indian middle class. This seems to be a universal phenomenon. Pol Pot very well realised that it is the middle class that shapes the societal mind; it constitutes it. He wanted to eliminate any element of dissent from the middle class. About the systematic and sustained blows on middle class, Ghosh writes, 'Cambodia's was not a civil war in the same sense as Somalia's or the former Yugoslavia's, fought over the fetishism of small difference: it was a war on history itself, an experiment in the re-invention of society. No regime in history had ever before made so systematic an attack on the middle class. Yet, if the experiment was proof of anything at all, it was ultimately of the indestructibility of the middle class, of its extraordinary tenacity and resilience; its capacity to preserve its forms of knowledge and expression through the most extreme kinds of adversity' (10).

Chea-Samy's personal connection with Pol Pot also has an interesting story. It is through her we get the famous lines of Pol Pot, 'The Revolution does not recognize families.' During his regime he bestowed no favours on members of his family, not even Chea-Samy's husband who was Pol Pot's elder brother. When king Sisobath died in 1927, his son Monivong became the king. But his love for his favourite mistress Luk Khun Meak changed everything. The palace in Phnom Penh and its regime underwent complete change. In place of princess Soumphady, Meak became the supervisor of all girl folk. Meak knew how to exercise her power. She brought many of her relatives to the palace and gave them important charges. One of her young relatives later became Chea-Samy's husband. Her husband's youngest brother was a six-year-old boy called Saloth Sar. He was later to become the terror god of Cambodia, Pol Pot. But what Chea-Samy says almost amounts to irony for us, 'He was a very good boy, she said at last, emphatically. In all the years he lived with me, he never gave me any trouble at all' (13).

It only goes on to show the mystery of human nature. It is so difficult to get hold of the particular thing that actually makes a dictator, a dictator, a terrorist, a terrorist, and a bandit, a bandit. Except for the inerasable impression of his childhood on his mind, Pol Pot does not seem to have anything away from the normal. He was a boy who 'gave no trouble at all.' And yet this boy got two million people butchered! Ghosh hints at problems that arose out of France's colonization of Cambodia. Khmer, as we have already noted, is one powerful tribe of Cambodia. These groups resorted to Guerrilla war tactics. Pol Pot's tactics was simply breeding hatred his target was Vietnam and Cambodia's own Vietnamese minority, Ghosh suggests that the fact that Pol Pot lived the formative years of his life in the 'elitist, racially exclusive culture of the court' might have had a permanent impact on him. Ghosh also cites historian Ben Kiernan in this regard. An overdose of ideology of national and racial grandiosity might have damaged Pol Pot's thinking. This man was an unashamed racist. As Ghosh described the reaction of one Khmer Rouge detectors, 'As far as the Vietnamese are concerned, whenever we meet them, whether they are militaries or civilians, because they are not ordinary civilians but soldiers disguised as civilians, we must kill them, whether they are men, women or children, there is no distinction, 'they are enemies' (25).

Ghosh also explains how terror was essential to the exercise of power by Khmer Rouge. All the old comrades were executed for betraying the Revolution. Pol Pot's ally Khieu Samplion planned 'the mass purges of the period,' meaning thereby the killings. They had ideas like purging the land of all sinners. They believed in a moral, religious tone of their activities, 'Terror was essential to their exercise of power. It was an integral part not merely of their coercive machinery, but of the moral order on which they built their regime' (50). As someone has said that human beings commit crimes so happily in the name of religion. Pol Pot's hero was Robespierre. What he loved most about this terror icon from France was his line, 'Terror is an emanation of virtue' (50). The author systematically goes on to show how the Revolution began to devour Itself. But it did not end before damaging Cambodia so badly.

It was in 1975 that Khmer Rouge seized power. (chea-Samy goes on to describe how she and her husband, like everyone else, were forced to go to serve in a village of old people. The Khmer Rouge loyalists along with the new converts were made to work in rice fields. For two years, there was complete 'news blackout' in Cambodia. No one knew as to what was happening.

Keeping the people in dark was one of the ways of terror mechanics of Khmer Rouge. It was only in 1978, the terror organization started building personality cult around its leader. Actually their fall was imminent and inevitable. Just to save themselves from collapsing, this building of personality cult was their last desperate move. Ghosh writes, 'Chea-Samy was working in a communal kitchen at the time, cooking and washing dishes. Late that year (1978) some party workers stuck a poster on the walls of the kitchen: they said it was a picture of their leader, Pol Pot. She knew who it was the moment she set eyes on the picture. That was how she discovered that the leader of the terrible, inscrutable organization Angkar, that ruled over their lives was none other than little Saloth Sar' (14).

When Vietnamese broke Cambodia in 1979, the country became 'like a shattered slate,' before you could think of drawing lines on it, you had to find pieces and fit them together' (16). And what actually did the fitting in was nothing else but the traditional Cambodian art forms. We usually do not give much importance to music and dance in our day-to-day prosaic lives. But music lies deep in human psyche. Only reading this book is believing this truth. It is a wonder how Ghosh creates the impact of music on the mind of the reader through this book. I, for one, will always welcome Cambodian music. In the post-revolution period, the Cambodian ministry of culture launched a project to relocate and gather the trained classical dancers and teachers. The results of this search were shocking. Almost ninety per cent of the artists had been killed in the Pol Pot regime. Anyone who survived found living to be a miracle. If one dancer found out another dancer they would shout, 'you are still alive!' And then they would cry thinking of all those who had died. One well-known surviving dancer described her condition during the Pol Pot time, 'I was like a smoker who gives up smoking [...]. I would dream of dance when I was alone or at night. You could get through the day because of the hard work. It was the nights that were really difficult; we would lie awake wondering who was going to be called out next. That was when I would dance, in my head' (16).

As I said, reading this book is believing the worth of art. Ghosh describes the worth of art. Ghosh describes the response of a Catholic relief worker from Italy, Onesta Carpen. When first music concert was organized, there was electricity crisis, 'The city was in shambles; there was debris everywhere, spilling out of the houses, on to the pavements, the streets were jammed with pillaged cars, there was no money and very little food. 'I could not believe that in a situation like that people would be thinking of music and dance. But still they come pouring in and theatre was filled far beyond its capacity. It was very hot inside' (52). Another foreigner Eva Mysliviec, a Quaker relief missionary, who also witnessed the first performance, recalls it thus, 'when the musicians came on the stage she heard sobs all around her. Then, when the dancers appeared, in their shabby, hastily made costumes, suddenly everyone was crying—people wept through the entire length of the performance' (52).

Here music and dance stand for life itself. It is as though the collective Cambodian voice is saying, 'to live is to sing and dance.' The sudden and spontaneous bouts of joy only strengthen the belief that artistic heritage is the very life and soul of a nation. The tears at the first performance are the tears of finding life again. It is as though. 'I'd thought I'd died but no, I'm alive I'm living.' In fact Ghosh develops the passion for dance and music as symbols of politics of resurgence in Cambodia. These art forms gave the beleaguered Cambodian people an identity and certitude, a badge of authenticity. The author sums up the mood as 'a kind of rebirth: a moment when the grief of survival became indistinguishable from the joy of living' (52).

When as a reader, I thought about the power of Ghosh in conveying so successfully the multiplicity and depth of life, I came to realize that he did it because the voices that he heard and noted were those of women. In situations like the Pol Pot regime, women suffer more simply because in the 'animal' scheme of things, women become the 'weaker' sex. Ghosh's identification with Chea-Samy and friends is complete. He trusts their version and suffers like them while listening the horror tales. That is why he succeeds in narration. To sympathize and empathise with women needs a special kind of sensitivity because here the normal parameters of power and success do not matter; what matters is acceptance. Womanhood, as has been described by some philosophers, is a state of 'being' while manhood is that of 'becoming.' While manhood implies effort and achievement, womanhood means 'being' what you are. It is only when complete osmosis has been achieved with the state of being that one gets a feel of life, 'real' life. But I cannot go into the philosophical depths and differences among various schools here. What I suggest is simply that Ghosh's contact with the old ladies gives him better understanding. Ladies like Chea-Samy are the real heroines. Ghosh writes, 'Like everyone around her, Chea-Samy too had started all over again—at the age of sixty, with her health shattered by the years of famine and hard labour. Working with quite, dogged persistence, she and a handful of other dancers and musicians slowly brought together a ragged, half starved bunch of orphans and castaways, and with the discipline of their long, rigorous years of training they began to resurrect the art that princess Soumphady and Luk Khun Meak had passed on to them in that long ago world, when king Sisobath reigned. Out of the ruins around them they began to create the means of denying Pol Pot his victory' (18).

In such touching passages, along with the power of womanhood, we also get the message of the worth of the old people. They are the living reservoirs of past. They are living tradition. They are the solid ground on which we today stand and jump and try to catch the stars. In moments of crisis, they can provide all that, we think, has been lost to us.

The social and political history of Cambodia from 1906 to 1993 has been narrated with an added human dimension. Both the dates are important. In 1906 Cambodian performers went to Europe for showing their native skills. These native skills will, in future give them strength to live and dream. 1993 is the year when finally under the auspices of the UN's Transitional Authority of Cambodia, country wide elections were held.

The second chapter of this book is devoted to the description of various aspects of the twelfth century Cambodian temple Angkor Wat. This temple is actually much more than a temple in the traditional sense to Cambodians. Many stories are carved on these elegant structures. Cambodians call Angkor Wat, 'A Monument to the Power of the Story.' This monument is sort of a gigantic abacus of story telling. It is a big, huge architectural device. It is said to be the largest single religious edifice in the world. It seems to be self-sufficient and complete in its setting and dimensions where each part is complementing the other. The setting is Mountain Meru. It is a mountain in Indian mythology. The seven graded tiers of the mythological hill provide the blue print for Angkor Wat. The entire pantheon of gods, deities, sages and prophets is cast.

We are pleasantly surprised that Ghosh offers one of his own discoveries regarding the temple. Ghosh says that he noticed the paradoxical nature of the reputation this temple has among Cambodians and the people of the rest of the world. People around the globe view Angkor Wat as a unique powerful symbol of the romance and glory of a lost civilization. But for Cambodians, it is a symbol of modernity. Although Angkor Wat is undisputedly a temple, yet it does not figure in anything that has to do with religion or any thing old-fashioned. Many factory-produced commodities bear it as a logo. It is stamped on uniforms. '[...] It figures on the logos of large corporations, like bank, indeed, the erstwhile Kampuchea Airlines even succeeded in transforming this most earth bound of structures into a symbol of flight, by lending it a pair of wings' (56).

Ghosh's training as an anthropologist really helps him here. He comes to know about the legend of accidental finding of this temple by French explorer Henri Mohout. It is one of those types of miracle stories where structures are supposed to have come up. The contradictory nature of this temple further gets a boost when Ghosh comes to know how this temple was restored with all latest available scientific and technical methods. Indian archaeologists were also called for help. Thus this central cultural symbol of Cambodia is also a symbol of change and modernity. Ghosh writes, 'For an entire generation of Cambodians, including politicians as different in ideology as Prince Sihanouk, Son Sann and Pol Pot, Angkor Wat became a symbol of modernizing nation-state. It became the opposite of itself: [an icon that represented a break with the past—a token of the country's belongings, not within the medieval, but rather the contemporary world. Thus, the bear, banks, airlines and of course flags' (60).

Decolonization is essentially a process of confusion and uncertainties. Post-colonial countries that wish to decolonise their mind-set face many challenges. In getting reactionary against the erstwhile colonizer, they run the risk of forming wrong judgments. These countries also face recolonisation in form of globalization and commercialization. These countries, on one hand, go for extreme glorification of their past and yet on the other hand, wish to compete in today's globalized world. Ghosh's description of Cambodian intellectual crisis applies to India as well. Seeking refuge in past glories to compensate for today's inadequacies is a recurrent feature of many newly liberated states. I remember Naipaul's Nobel lecture where he says that the colonized lie about themselves. Their talking falsely big about themselves and feeling great is their only weapon. In my view, getting 'mad' about decolonization will not lead us anywhere. The other day I was talking to a very reputed Ramayana scholar from our region who has published some standard books on the subject. I said to him that one person who did not get justice in Rama Rajya was Sita. She was punished for a crime she did not commit. Rama deserted her when she needed him most, when she was carrying. She was the first victim of character assassination, a potent tool against women in our society. The old gentleman somehow, took upon himself to justify Rama's behaviour with the obvious presumption that whatever is Indian is good or even, whatever is good is bound to be Indian. I have seen and heard professors who claim that Sanskrit is the origin of Arabic, Persian and even French and English. One just cannot go with irrationality. What is happening actually is that this 'decolonization mania' is harming academic standards. There is lots of inbreeding. You read Indians, you apply Indians. So I, for one, ask for fresh air from all sides. Let us think in terms of having the best of both the worlds.

But I think I have gone a little far because Ghosh does not seem to imply so much. If anything, he is to be taken as a writer with a decolonized bent of mind. He only suggests here that in the process of decolonization an exaggerated thrust is given on past glories.

The last part of the book 'At Large in Burma' is mostly a linear narrative. As expected, its topic is struggle for democracy in Burma. But Ghosh has a personal link to Burma as well. He says that writing about Burma is an attempt on his part to get at his roots. He wants to explore places his parents and relatives had lived in or visited before the birth of the Indian Republic in 1947. He writes, 'To me, the most intriguing of these stories were those that my family carried out of Burma. I suspect that this was partly because Burma had become a kind of lost world in the early 60's, when I was old enough to listen to my relatives' stories. It was in 1962 that General Ne win, the man who would be Burma's long time dictator, seized power in coup. Almost immediately, he slammed the shutters and switched off the lights: Burma became the dark house of the neighbourhood, huddled behind an impenetrable, overgrown fence. It was to remain shuttered for almost three decades' (65).

In his family, memories of Burma were kept alive by an aunt and her husband nicknamed Prince who left Burma in 1942 and came to Calcutta just before the invasion of Rangoon by the Japanese army.

Basically, at the time of author's visit to Burma and even prior to that, two forces were working in Burma—forces of orthodoxy and *status quo* represented by the army and democratic forces, seeking change that have been headed by Nobel Peace Prize winner Aung San Suu Kyi. Suu Kyi's father Aung San was Burma's acknowledged leader during the freedom struggle. On 19th July 1947 he was assassinated. At the time of her father's death, Suu Kyi was just two years old. She rose to be an eminent human rights activist and spearheaded a peaceful non-resistance mass movement to restore democracy and civil liberties in her country. At the time of the author's visit she was still under house arrest. Ghosh analyses the political situation in today's world. Politics goes by symbols. If you have strong symbols, you will remain in public memory, otherwise not. He correctly writes, 'In the post-modern world, politics is everywhere a matter of symbol and the truth is that Suu Kyi is her own greatest political asset. It is only because Burma's 1988 democracy movement had a symbol, personified in Suu Kyi, that the world remembers it and continues to exert pressure on the current regime. Otherwise, the world would almost certainly have forgotten Burma's slain and dispersed democrats just as quickly as it has forgotten many others like them in the past' (83).

We can easily find parallels in Nelson Mandela being Africa's symbol in its anti-apartheid movement and Gandhi being our own symbol of freedom and self-reliance. How strange that collective anguish must find one universally accepted voice to be taken notice of. Ghosh is also conscious of the double standards adopted by erstwhile colonizers and developed nations. In theory they support democracy, freedom of speech and liberty for people of all races, but for political and economic gain support dictatorial and terrorism inclined regimes. Burma has been fighting civil wars since its Independence in January 1948. There has been a communist uprising. Military coups have decided the order of the day. Ghosh tries to analyze as to what went wrong in Burma and where did thing go wrong? It used to be one of the richest countries in Asia and yet now it lists in UN's ten least developed nations on earth. Burma has become the byword for repression, xenophobia and civil abuse. About two third of the country's population is Buddhist. But during the colonial rule, Britishers favoured minorities over ethnic Burmans. Even the army had units names after the minorities like 'Karen' Rifles, 'Shan,' Mon and so on. But things were to change and change for better, 'It takes a military dictator to believe that symbols are inert and can be manipulated at will. Forty years after his assassination, Aung San had his revenge. In a strange, secular reincarnation, his daughter Suu Kyi, came back to haunt those who had sought to make use of his death. In 1988, when Burma's decades of discontent culminated in an anti-military uprising, Aung San Suu Kyi emerged from obscurity as one of country's most powerful voices, the personification of Burma's democratic resistance to military rule' (74).

Without undermining Suu Kyi's greatness, we can also see the role of circumstances and the times in creating a great personality. Suu Kyi is a product and a necessity of the age in which she is placed. We, Indians, very well know her tools—non-violence, peaceful resistance. Ghosh realizes how popular this frail lady is. She held rallies at her residence. She answered questions ranging from food and health to politics and literature. The only reason how the army succeeded in grabbing power for so long is its wide and deep surveillance system. Suu Kyi is meek, conciliatory and patient. But she is not weak. Her firm belief that sooner or later, the army rule would go is amazing.

She tells Ghosh, 'I have always told you [...] that we will win [...] that we will establish a democracy in Burma and I stand by that, but as to when, I cannot predict. I've always said that to you' (113-14).

Now that we know the events of later years, we can only say that Suu Kyi's conviction was correct.

REFERENCE

Ghosh, Amitav. 1998. *Dancing in Combodia, At Large in Burma*. New Delhi: Ravi Dayal Publisher.

7
Countdown

Countdown, a small book of 106 pages with 13 unmarked chapters exposes the nuclear lobby in India as well as Pakistan. It is a spontaneously written book. The occasion of writing it is India's nuclear explosion test on 11th May 1998, followed promptly by the Pakistani tests. Ghosh visits Pokharan in Rajasthan, the site of tests, Siachen glacier at India-Pakistan border and then finally Pakistan. He talks to many people and forms his impressions on nuclear testing. People of Pokharan are full of grief and sorrow when they recount their horrendous and horrifying experiences regarding nuclear testing. Ghosh feels that reasons behind this nuclear testing are not related to the security of either nation. It is indeed sad to note that our region is dominated by 'stunt' politics, which seldom cares for the peace and prosperity of people. The book grows into a mild satire on this petty politics. The book does not miss on Pakistan's poor social, political, economical and religious conditions.

The author went to Pokharan three months after the tests. The book opens with an apocalyptic vision of the Pokharan site. Ghosh openly satirizes the celebration held to celebrate the great day. Party workers and sympathizers distributed sweets to people. They even talked of sending dust from Pokharan to different parts of India as sacred soil. They wanted to build a sort of a monument of strength at the site. Even the Prime Minister is not left unscathed by Ghosh. 'On 15 May, four days after the test [...] a celebration was organized on the crater left by the blasts. The Prime Minister was photographed standing on the crater's ruin, throwing flowers into the pit. It was as though this were one of the crowning achievements of his life' (6). But people in and around Pokharan are not happy for obvious reasons. Manohar Joshi, one of the first journalists to know about the tests, says, 'In the years after 1974 there was so much illness here that people didn't have money to buy pills. We had never heard of cancer before in this area. But people began to get cancer after test. There were strange skin diseases. People used to scratch themselves all the time' (7). Many other people of Pokharan tell Ghosh about the birth of deformed children, growth of tumor in cows and birth of blind and deformed calves. It is so tragic to learn how politicians, be it in 1974 or 1998, for their selfish interests, play with the lives of people. As King Lear says, 'What flies to wanton boys, are we to gods. They kill us for their sport.' How it suits the visionless leadership of India. As one parliamentarian tells Ghosh that the explosions were done to save the government from exploding from within; to quiet voices of dissent from within the coalition government. Still, many sleep in this country without food. Floods and famines are a regular feature. There is no comprehensive plan to deter these annual natural calamities. All that we are doing is adding to them by nuclear testing. For one single battle tank, one hundred schools could be opened in rural areas. And yet our annual defense budget is well above thirty five thousand crores of rupees.

Had this mind-boggling expenditure been for defending the country, it would have been okay. But it is not so. As a noted defense affairs expert, K. Subrahmanyam tells the author, 'Nuclear weapons are the currency of global power. Nuclear weapons are not military weapons' (13). Ghosh goes on to prove that these tricks are nothing but post colonialism of the perverted order. The fifty years of unfulfilled promises, the frustration of not being able to realise potential, the growing corruption—all these find a temporary atonement in such exercises. We can take a cricket match as a fine analogy. Defeat Pakistan and all the ills of this country vanish into a momentary euphoria. But nuclear testing is no cricket match. It is a very costly and more dangerous ploy to build our lost self-respect and nationalistic mood. As Chandan Mitra, the historian tells Ghosh that with two hundred years of colonization India has lost national cohesion. With loss of self-esteem, the bomb has become a symbol of self-esteem. It is the global currency with which India wants to be a player, a manipulator of the international order. But according to Ghosh, India's nuclear programme is like minting false coins to purchase 'world-wide influence.' The message is clear that we can become influential only by sorting out our real problems like population, poverty, unemployment and corruption and not by these cheap (or not so cheap) stunts. Ghosh uses the discussion to show the wrong direction of our decolonization. For him, it only symbolizes the complexive mindset of the still not mentally decolonized people of India. The bomb is a false symbol of re-arrangement of global power, a political insurgency or any kind of millenary movement.

Countdown is a kind of shock for readers of Ghosh. He has always been an author, disagreeing with the British and the Western world in its treatment of India. His writings always depicted double standards shamelessly followed by the controlling powers of the world. But here he takes an introspective look. He is viewing Indians rather ruthlessly. But then, why not? Self-criticism can always lead to healthier attitudes and better practices. It is in this spirit, I take this book although I must admit that it is depressing in its effect. The book succeeds in showing the mess in which we have placed our country. It boldly points out the glaring leadership crisis in India. We have politicians, but we do not have leaders. In fact, about thirty or so pages of this book deal with the author's visit to Siachen with the defense minister of India. The author reminds the minister of his earlier involvement with anti-nuclear writings and peace-marches. But in the typical fashion of a politician, the minister says that although a bomb is morally unacceptable to him, yet India should keep all the options open and so on. The author feels that the minister is only lip-serving. Ghosh cannot conceal his severe disappointment when he says that one day we will sink, not because of Pakistan or China but because of our own putting up with apathetic leadership. What is implied is that we do not care for our country. And let me say that these comments do not come from an Asian American standing on a high pedestal but from someone among us. Ghosh's sincerity cannot be doubted.

Anyway to go with the line of the book, Ghosh describes the condition of soldiers deployed in very difficult places like Siachen Glacier, Leh, Ladakh and Suronk. Nature is indeed cruel at these places. With rising hostilities on the border these soldiers face the double threat of natural calamities on one hand and bullets on the other. The cost of maintaining these soldiers at these places is again shocking. But what is even more shocking is that the soldiers of the two countries are not very hostile or bitter in their words and approach to each other. Although the term 'Dushman' (enemy) is used but the Indian soldiers always spoke of their Pakistani counterparts with detachment and respect. Ghosh did not hear any verbal abuse. It only shows that soldiers do not want wars. But one army officer horrified Ghosh with his plan for winning the supposed war at Siachen Glacier, 'A nuclear explosion, inside the glacier, a mile deep. The whole thing would melt and the resulting flood would carry Pakistan away and also put an end to the glacier. We can work wonders' (43).

When Ghosh crosses the border and meets people in Pakistan, he finds starker belligerence there. In his interview the leader of Jamaat-e-Islami, Qazi Hussain Ahmed, very readily expresses the possibility of a nuclear war Ghosh says, 'In India I met very few people including anti-nuclear activists—who believe that a nuclear war might actually occur in the subcontinent. In Pakistan the opposite was to be. Almost everyone I met thought that nuclear war almost certainly lay ahead, somewhere down the road' (62). Qazi Hussain Ahmed even goes on justifying his stance by saying that no nation can have monopoly over scientific knowledge and technology. He says that with ever-increasing hatred between the two nations and with a history of wars who can deny the possibility of a nuclear war. He says that a nation would do anything to spare itself the shame of losing a war. The repulsion at such irresponsible comments is very clear. Ghosh quotes a member of a group called international physicians for the prevention of nuclear war, 'In the event of a nuclear explosion [...] the ones who will be alive will be jealous of the dead ones' (102).

Any sensitive human being would be horrified at the extent of indifference regarding human welfare among people of this sub-continent. People talk of nuclear weapons and wars as though they are talking about fairy tales. Leaders go for nuclear testing to get the votes. Ghosh cites the opinions of scientists like Raja Ramanna on the impact of a nuclear holocaust. It is indeed terrifying to imagine the destruction that such an explosion will cause in densely populated cities like Mumbai, Karachi, Delhi and Lahore. Ghosh also meets liberal activists in Pakistan like Asma Jahangir. She tells Ghosh about the hostility that she received from her own countrymen when she defended the human rights of religious minorities in Pakistan. She was held like a demon engaged in blasphemy against the holy prophet. She also feels that the two countries are engaged in an unnecessary and imaginary race. She rightly feels that the policies of the two countries are irrational and *ad hoc*. There is lots of false propaganda. She almost sounds desperate in her hope, 'I think once you break the barriers of disinformation, people's own instincts are what we have to depend on. I feel hopeful' (81).

For Ghosh, as for any thinking Indian, India-Pakistan relations have always been intriguing. He wanted to have a first hand experience of the people's expression. He says, 'I wanted to hear them for myself. What I heard instead was for the most part a strange mixture of psycholozing, grandiose fantasy and cynicism, allied with the deliberate conjuring up of illusory threats and imaginary fears. The truth is that India's nuclear program is status driven, not threat driven [...]. In Pakistan's case too the motivation behind the nuclear program [...] is parity with India. That the leaders of these two countries should be willing to run the risk of nuclear accidents, war and economic breakdown in order to indulge these confused ambitions is itself a sign that some essential element in the social compart has broken down: that there is no longer any commensurability between the desires of the rulers and the well being of the ruled. The pursuit of nuclear weapons in subcontinent is the moral equivalent of civil war: the targets the rulers have in mind for these weapons are, in the end, none other than their own people' (106).

Countdown is a deeply psychologically revealing analysis of the attitudes that lead to extreme animosity, abhorrence and suspicion between these two neighbouring countries. The politicians want to avert every future crisis by building an atmosphere of war and hatred for the neighbouring nation. Had it not been for the sophisticated and soft use of humorous language by Ghosh, this book could have been a literal lashing for everyone in India and Pakistan. Ghosh punctures the false ego. Our thinking is that we have tried everything to improve the conditions but all in vain, so this war (nuclear or cultural) with the neighbour is our last chance. We are actually getting desperate in our attitudes.

REFERENCE

Ghosh, Amitav. 1999. *Countdown*. New Delhi: Ravi Dayal Publisher.

8

The Glass Palace

The Glass Palace is comparatively a thicker book, not because Ghosh has changed his style or subject matter but because the narrative is extended up to three generations. This is, once again, a book about geographical entities, space, distance and time. Many stories have been woven together. There are many characters. It is a saga of many families, their lives and their connection with each other. To take this book in its entirety and comment on it, is not an easy task. But to begin with the beginning, we can say that this novel of Amitav Ghosh is the story of an Indian orphan who is transported to Burma by accident. The name of this character is Raj Kumar. As a child, Raj Kumar is remarkable for his exploring spirit, keen perception and his ability to take calculated risks. Raj Kumar works in a tea stall of a matronly lady Ma Cho. He loves exaggerating his age just of feel like an adult. A well-travelled orphan, Raj Kumar is worldly-wise. Right at the beginning of the narrative, the author drops enough hints for the legitimacy of his choice of a protagonist. Although, a child, an orphan, yet this boy is established as bold, and remarkable. Once Raj Kumar lands in Mandalay, his life-long search for places and people begins. He is taken in by the city. 'Long straight roads radiated outwards from the walls, forming a neat geometrical grid. So intriguing was the ordered pattern of these streets that Raj Kumar wandered far a field, exploring' (5). And we must remember that this exploring boy is a complete destitute in an alien city with absolutely no acquaintances. Finally he goes to Ma Cho for job and he receives a thorough rebuke and scolding at the very outset. But his keen perception helps him to know 'that' this outburst was not aimed directly at him: that it had more to do with the dust, the splattering oil and the price of vegetables than with his own presence or with anything he had said' (5-6).

Ghosh is a master at pointing out small details that actually make the characters and the narrative real. Soon the boy Raj Kumar develops his sense of belonging at the new place. Barriers are challenging to him. In fact, barriers cause progress. If there would be no hurdles, who would think of ascending and getting beyond. As he views the fort of Mandalay the crystal shining glass palace, he instinctively knows that orphans like him cannot go there and yet 'No matter what Ma Cho said, he decided, he would cross the moat—before he left Mandalay, he would find a way in' (7). It is this spark that sets Raj Kumar apart for a life of success, adventure and prosperity.

His lessons of worldly wisdom come soon. With no one to guide or look after him, he goes where his fancy takes him. Through the creaks in the wooden walls, he starts viewing Ma Cho at nights. He gets to know about female anatomy and sex in this way. He even gets his first physical sensations through Ma Cho, though fortunately she does not go beyond limits and resists herself well in time. It is pathetic to watch the condition of an orphan growing boy whose only tutor is life. He is just a toy and Ma Cho could have made him whatever she wanted. But 'abruptly, she pushed him away, with a yelp of disgust. What am I doing with this boy, this child, this half-wit kalaa? Elbowing him aside, she clambered up her ladder and vanished into her room' (57).

Once again the sanity of the situation is saved by a woman's strength. I have been watching this pattern quite regularly in Ghosh's works where animality is more or less left to men and women save the grace of human existence.

It is at this roadside tea stall only, Raj Kumar meets the man in Ma Cho's life, Saya John. Saya John comes closest to what Raj Kumar could have called a father. But this does not come in a day. Raj Kumar matures fast. Life teaches him its own lessons. At his heart, he is always certain about his success in life. When the British throw down the king of Burma, Raj Kumar is told that the British wish to control Burmese territory for wood. And from this point starts his shaping of his future plans. He senses wealth in teak. When the city is rampaged by the British, it is the Indian soldiers who come on orders of their colonial masters. Suddenly Indians become the target of mob frenzy. Raj Kumar is also attacked. He is saved by Saya John. That day, Saya perceives something unique in Raj Kumar. 'There was something unusual about the boy—a kind of watchful determination. No excess of gratitude here, no gifts or offerings, no talk of honour, with murder in the heart. There was no simplicity in his face, no innocence: his eyes were filled with worldliness, curiosity, and hunger. That was as it should be.

'If you ever need a job,' Saya John said, 'come and talk to me' (3).

We can say that Raj Kumar earns his job at Saya's company with his integrity and personality. But his learning process is far from over. When the palace of King Thebaw is evacuated, everyone rushes into it to loot as much as they can. Raj Kumar also goes in. But what he gets there is not an item of loot but his future wife Dolly. Dolly like Raj Kumar is an orphan. She is a maid who looks after the princesses. At that tender age Raj Kumar is struck by this girl. He offers her some sweets. Soon he sees her sharing those sweets with a soldier. Raj Kumar feels angry but soon learns a lesson 'Dolly was doing exactly what had to be done. What purpose would it serve for these girls to make a futile show of resentment? How could they succeed in defiance when the very army of the realm had succumbed?' (46). This is how Raj Kumar's life goes. He learns from experiences. He is receptive. He is forming friendships that will endure for generations. He is learning to see the world not only through his own eyes but also as others see it. Saya is his tutor for all practical purposes. When Saya is rebuked by an English boss, Raj Kumar flares up. It is Saya that passes his wisdom to Raj Kumar, literally teaches him to see the other side of a picture. Through these poignant phases, Raj Kumar grows. When Saya earnestly tells Raj Kumar how to live, how to deal with people and situations, once his orphanhood strikes him right at heart, 'Raj Kumar could tell that Saya John was thinking not of him [...] but of Mathew, his absent son and the realisation brought a sudden and startling pang of grief. But the pain lasted only an instant and when it had faded Raj Kumar felt himself to be very much the stronger, better prepared' (75).

His being an orphan gives him a unique sensibility. He is able to watch every scene with detachment. His only concern, pure and simple, is to defend himself and provide for himself. He is a growing boy, without strings. It is a disadvantage but then it is an advantage as well. Or we may say that Raj Kumar takes this negative fact in his stride and makes good use of it. It makes him what he is—practical. 'He reserved his trust and affection for those who earned it by concrete example and proven good will [...]. But that there should exist a universe of loyalities that was unrelated to himself and his own immediate needs—this was very nearly incomprehensible' (47). So this attitude of Raj Kumar leaves out all loyalities related to place, nationhood etc. He is free.

He uses this free will in building his business. His professional rise is impressive. When he decides to take a loan from Saya and establish his separate timber yard, Saya is full of doubts. Now it is Raj Kumar's turn to give a few tips to Saya, 'If I'm ever going to make this business grow, I'll have to take a few risks' (130). With risks he grows and grows very well. By the time Raj Kumar is ripe to go to India to search Dolly, he is already a successful and respected businessman. Tracing Dolly is not difficult because she has been with the deposed King and Queen of Burma.

Being a practical businessman, Raj Kumar brings with him a letter for the Collector of Ratangiri from a relative of the Collector's wife Uma Dey. Usually no one from Burma is allowed to meet the deposed king or staff lest such a meeting may not create problems of revolt at Burma. Uma, who is a good friend of Dolly arranges the meeting between Dolly and Raj Kumar. But before going to that, the letter of endorsement that Raj Kumar brought with him speaks volumes about his character and reputation. '[...] he (Raj Kumar) had several other successes and had risen to eminence within the business community. And all this at the age of thirty, before he had even had time to marry '[...]. Raj Kumar babu is not the kind of person to whose society you are accustomed. You may well find him somewhat rough and even uncouth in his manner [...]. But here in Burma our standards are a little more lax. Some of the richest people in the city are Indians and most of them began with nothing more than a bundle of clothes and a tin box' (135).

Raj Kumar is an individual here as well as a representative, a symbol of a whole migrated community. His fate and rise have been linked to that of his community and what we get in a wonderful individual picturisation as well as functioning of an entire group of people in an alien land. This is what I call flashes of genius on part of the author.

Raj Kumar's meeting with Dolly is catastrophic. There is no clue, no meeting point, no headway. It is all blocked, clogged. Dolly has her own problems. She has to clear her mental picture. But this we shall discuss later while talking about Dolly. For no fault of his, Raj Kumar receives a cold and hostile response from Dolly. His dreams are all but broken. As fate would have it, they are married at Ratangiri. Uma is their benefactor, protector, everything. They would not have been married but for the Collector's wife Uma Dey. From here begins Raj Kumar's life as a family man. He gets two sons Neel and Dinu. He celebrates to compensate for all the missed celebrations of his own life. But his life cannot be called perfect as he falls prey to the turbulent times in his old age and his world is torn apart. Dinu moves away from him, Neel dies and Dolly goes to a monastery. Although the end can be blamed at fate, one flaw is very much Raj Kumar's own. Once Dinu as a child develops slight polio in one leg. Dolly consumes herself day and night in Dinu's care. She becomes more and more introvert. She cuts herself off from the world, including her elder son, Neel and husband. Dinu and his well being remain the focal point of her existence for months or even a year or so. It is as though the mother and the son have reentered the prenatal period of oneness. The child is safely in mother's protective presence, her womb and all his needs are fulfilled without asking. During this period Raj Kumar goes into physical relationship with one of the workers forcibly and Ilongo, his illegitimate son is the result of this extramarital mating. We can only attribute this act on Raj Kumar's part to his free will and the kind of a man that he actually is. Saya, his mentor, was the same and so is he. Our civilised and often hypocritical rules of morality will not work here simply because this novel, like other good novels, is a true depiction of life. Howsoever absurd such an act may look to the cold, distant gaze, it is perhaps the most natural thing to happen in the mess of life. Devoid of the power of reasoning as to why Dolly has withdrawn, Raj Kumar succumbs to his physical needs. He remains, despite his achievements, an uneducated orphan.

Dolly is initially Queen Supayalat's maid who later grows into her own person. It is actually Dolly's contact with Uma Dey that ripens her and gives her a personality. Dolly is beautiful, even more beautiful than the princesses that she attends. Basically it is this extraordinary beauty that enforces a sort of depth on her. Not everyone is able to manage beauty,

I mean, extraordinary beauty. Beauty attracts. Beauty demands protection. Beauty also demands graceful behaviour, lest it may be marred. Well, Dolly fulfills many prerequisites of beauty if not all. Her life is intertwined with the life of King and

Queen. Dolly is introduced most casually just as an attendant, an attache to the bigger, larger, royal way of life. Dolly's speciality lies in her ability to calm the youngest princess who is extremely stubborn and cries and shouts on every possible occasion. Dolly, herself a child of ten, manages the youngest princess as best as she can. The scene where Dolly is not able to carry the young princess in her lap when the palace is ravaged is particularly touching because one individual's suffering looks so small and yet so poignant. 'I can't, she cried. I, can't. She would fall, she knew it. The princess was too heavy for her; the stairs were too high; she would need a free hand to hold on, to keep her balance [...] Quickly, quickly. There was a soldier behind her; he was prodding her with the cold hilt of his sword. She felt her eyes brimming over, tears flooding down her face. Couldn't they see she would fall, that the Princess would tumble out of her grip? Why would no one help? (23).

These beginning pages of the novel juxtapose two aspects of female power so well. On one hand goes the story of queen Supayalat who is an expert in cruel court intrigues and palace politics and on the other hand a twelve years old boy offers sweets to a ten year old vulnerable girl. The contrast is too intense to be missed. Queen Supayalat is no ordinary woman. Thebaw is ineffectual and scholarly type of a person. But most unexpectedly Supayalat 'in defiance of the protocols of palace intrigue, fell headlong in love with her husband, the king. His ineffectual good nature seemed to inspire a maternal ferocity in her. In order to protect him from her family she stripped her mother of her powers and banished her to a corner of the palace, along with her sisters and co-wives. Then she set about ridding Thebaw of his rivals. She ordered the killing of every member of the Royal Family who might ever be considered a threat to her husband. Seventy-nine princes were slaughtered on her orders, some of them newborn infants and some too old to walk. To prevent the spillage of royal blood she had them wrapped in carpets and bludgeoned to death. The corpses were thrown into the nearest river' (38-39).

But the enigma of human nature is such that this most cruel person goes on to live in exile, suffers captivity and humiliation for love, for her husband. 'What could love mean to this woman, this murderer, responsible for the slaughter of scores of her own relatives? And yet it was a fact that she had chosen captivity over freedom for the sake of her husband, condemned her own daughters to twenty years of exile' (152).

It is not the duty of the novelist to solve all the puzzles of human nature; his work finishes with the candid presentation of them.

To come back to Dolly, she is steadfast in her loyalty to the royal family. She remains with them in the most critical circumstances. One by one all the maids and servants leave the royal family and go back to Burma but Dolly does not do so. This may partly be due to the fact that she has nowhere to go to. Yet the sincerity of her nature cannot be denied. Gradually from a child she becomes an attractive young girl. Her body and mind expand. She has nothing to look forward to. She cannot dream for herself. Her life is an appendage, a depending extension of the royal family. Sex comes as a handy rescue for this young girl to maintain her sanity. The novelist chooses to go in detail regarding Dolly's first exposure to the life of the body. Sawant is the local servant of the king. He is the chief servant. He is the natural choice for Dolly and she for him. But soon they are caught by the first Princess who herself is growing into a woman and is also in need of engagement of some sort. To cut a long tale short, the first princess snatches Sawant and her pregnancy is dramatically announced. By this time Collector Dey and his wife have arrived on the scene. The Collector is responsible for the well being of the royal family.

When Raj Kumar comes to take her, Dolly has run into a dead end. She is in an emotional chaos. She is not interested in Raj Kumar. By some sort of psychological transference, she identifies with the first princess and says that she is awaiting the baby's arrival. She feels the baby to be her own. But Uma knows better, 'the birth of this child will drive you out of your mind [...]' (163). Dolly's meeting with Raj Kumar is of great value in understanding the kind of a person she is. She is so clear in her perceptions. When Uma coaxes her to marry Raj Kumar and says that he loves her, Dolly's reply is remarkably correct, 'He's in love with what he remembers. That isn't me' (161). She goes on to tell Raj Kumar about her past relationship with Sawant. Finally, Raj Kumar and Dolly are married.

What is the charm of Dolly's personality? What makes her click? Uma herself confesses it to Dolly what she owes to her. Dolly is the personification of the spirit of endurance and acceptance. Her very weakness is her source of strength. Dolly yields. She gives in. And that is why she is so much in demand, sought after by Uma, Raj Kumar, Princesses, King, Queen, Sawant, just everyone. She reminds me of servant characters from the novels of Pearl S. Buck. There also, understanding and accepting place a servant on a greater pedestal than the angry wife.

Uma is another pillar of this novel. The power of Ghosh's narration is such that the moment Uma enters the novel, the reader knows that she has come to stay. The Collector and Uma go to the house of the King and Queen. The meeting is awkward and stiff. But Uma makes her mark. The Queen Supayalat is impressed by her. 'Self-possession was a quality she'd always admired. There was something attractive about this woman, Uma Dey; the liveliness of her manner was a welcome contrast to her husband's arrogance' (108).

Uma develops a close friendship with Dolly. Their friendship lasts a whole lifetime. But for all her sophistication, liveliness and charm, there are problems in Uma's life that she has not been able to sort out. The bond between her and her husband is weak. The Collector has been educated abroad. He does not fit into Indian scheme of things. The author makes an indirect comment on the state of Indian marriages when he says, 'the wifely virtues she could offer him he had no use for: Cambridge had taught him to want more, to make sure that nothing was held in abeyance, to bargain for a woman's soul with the coin of kindness and patience. The thought of this terrified her. This was subjection beyond decency, beyond her imagining. She could not bring herself to think of it. Anything would be better than to submit' (153).

And this exactly how it is with majority of Indian marriages. The couple lives together for decades without really knowing each other, without actually sharing innermost thoughts and without genuinely loving each other. Marriage becomes a matter of habit, a taken for granted ritual of life. The Collector wants mental connection with Uma. Her resources prove to be inadequate on this account. She does not love her husband. She does not trust him. She may be having 'wife virtues' namely timely supply of needs, patience, passivity etc. but a bond with the husband is something she dreads. The Collector, on the other hand is a different type of a man. We can say he is intellectually emancipated. He selected Uma after seeing her at a puja when she was sixteen. He wanted a flexible girl who is not too settled in her ideas and behaviour. His family opposed Uma. 'But he persisted, insisting that he didn't want a conventional marriage. He'd be working with Europeans: it wouldn't do to have a conservative, housebound wife. He needed a girl who would be willing to step out into society; someone young, who wouldn't be resistant to learning modern ways' (158).

But things turn out to be different. 'Disappointment' is the word that settles too soon in their relationship. Uma is leading a mechanical, lonely life playing the part of elegant hostess in all the social gathering of the Collector. It is Dolly who releases her from this chain of boredom and dull schedule. She connects well with Dolly. Her husband does not occupy her psychological space. Things are bound to fall apart. Once Dolly leaves, the

Collector is perceptive enough to say to Uma when she approaches him, 'You have come to tell me that you want to go home' (172). Uma has decided to leave the Collector. She has decided that she cannot go on like that. The dialogue that follows is touching and tragic. There can be nothing more sad in this world than talk of broken dreams. The Collector does exactly the same, 'I used to dream about the kind of marriage I wanted [...]. To live with a woman as an equal, in spirit and intellect: this seemed to me the most wonderful thing life could offer. To discover together the world of literature, art: what could be richer, more fulfilling? But what I dreamt is not yet possible, not here, in India, not for us' (173).

Uma leaves and the Collector goes to row out into the sea, never to return. He feels that there is no need to turn back home as no one would be waiting for him and he would find it hard to sleep. And thus goes a precious life, a talented, sensitive human life. The Collector commits suicide. He proves to be even more vulnerable than Uma.

And this is just the beginning of a series of tragic deaths in this novel. One thing that disturbs me in the novel is that there is hardly any poetic justice. The dead ones are left just like that. For example, with the Collector's death Uma's life takes an upward swing. She becomes a globetrotter, a freedom fighter and a sort of celebrity in her own right. Except for a passing remark that she mourned her husband's death for fifty years, there is hardly any real 'feel' of her sorrow. A tear somewhere, an ache in the heart, just anything to tell the reader that she is missing her husband or that she is repenting for her cruel treatment of the Collector would have been more satisfying. I read the whole novel to find something that would honour the Collector's memory but nothing came. Instead the novel distastefully ends in, 'But that morning when I (Raj Kumar's grand daughter) ran into Uma's room, I found, to my surprise, that Raj Kumar was in her bed. They were fast asleep, their bodies covered by a thin, cotton sheet. They looked peaceful and very tired, as though they were resting after some great exertion' (545).

The lines tell that Uma's image 'as a woman of icy selfcontainment, a widow who had mourned her dead husband, for more than half a century' was false. The reader is at a loss as to what to make of it. These lines even take away the edge from what Raj Kumar once told Uma earlier in their lives when they were young and sensible, 'Have you ever built anything? Given a single person a job? Improved anyone's life in any way? No. All you ever do is stand back, as though you were above all of us and you criticise and criticise. Your husband was as fine a man as any I've ever met and you hounded him to his death with your self-righteousness' (248).

The truth of these lines is self-evident. Even with these bitterly true words Uma does not go into any kind of selfquestioning. Well, all that I can say is that this amounts to a flaw to draw a character who is a celebrated international socialite and intellectual and yet who never goes into any kind of introspection. To me, Uma's characterisation looks unreal. Even to the crudest women, widowhood drives into bouts of loneliness and depression. The endless vacuum of life pervades their personality. How can an educated, sensitive, patriotic, modern lady escape an inevitable thought process?

To move over to other areas in this novel we may talk about the next generation. The children of Raj Kumar and Dolly, Saya John's grand children and Uma's nephew and nieces are no less interesting than their parents and aunts. Dinu, Dolly's younger son, is by far the most substantial figure in this group. He possesses a unique keenness. He is sharp. When Dinu is first taken seriously in this narrative, we again at once know that he is the hero of the later part of the novel. Dinu is instinctively thoughtful. He is not an extrovert. He is not very social even. Photography is his profession. When Dinu is an adolescent, Dolly encourages his interest in photography 'because she felt that she ought to encourage any activity that would draw him out of himself' (215). The natural inference that follows is that Dinu loves to remain within himself.

By the time the next generation arrives, the reader is into a web of relationships. The older generation is familiar. On that prior knowledge, the reader bases her/his opinions on the younger people. The importance of relationships is really so huge really in life. Without relationships, life would be meaningless. Uma alone is a detached observer of the scene. She feels that in the faces of these adolescents 'she could see inscribed the history of her friendships and the lives of her friends—the stories and trajectories that had brought Elsa's life into conjunction with Matthew's, Dolly's with Raj Kumar's, Malacca with New York, Burma with India' (225).

Dinu's behaviour as an adolescent says a lot about his personality in general. He is an expert at speaking bitter truths. He is not eloquent. Uma also realises his infatuation for Saya John's grand daughter Alison. Uma also notices the difference in their temperament. While Dinu is a boy of shadows, Alison is described as craving for spotlight. But the infatuation is there; it lasts till Alison's tragic death in world war.

We are reminded of Tridib's love for ruins in *The Shadow Lines* when Alison is also shown hooked by ruins. The older the ruin, the better. The author also delineates the psychology behind arranged marriages in India '[...] it was a way of shaping the future to the past, of cementing one's ties to one's memories and to one's friends' (230). Dinu's character is further delineated while his relationship with Alison is described. He cannot work unless he is fully dressed. He is not a casual type of a person. His keenness is also transferred to his perceptions. For example, as soon as he meets Ilongo, the son Raj Kumar had outside marriage, who is Dinu's half brother, Dinu immediately realises that between himself and Ilongo there existed some sort of connection—a link that was known to Ilongo but of which he himself was unaware' (359). This is no small achievement to realise connection with another person without any prior knowledge.

As a person of serious attitudes, Dinu's fall in love is also a very intentional and possessive business. We cannot say that he is totally successful here. His attraction for Alison is absolute. But once Arjun, Uma's nephew who is serving in Indian army, enters the scene, the equilibrium is lost. The liveliness of Alison matches with Arjun's power and for a short span of time Dinu loses Alison to Arjun. He is jealous of Arjun and his loud, impressive ways. He tries to come to terms with the situation. He knows that Alison cannot be trusted with Arjun. But he just can not do anything about it. He has only his inner resources. He decides not to fall a prey to self-pity. Alison, on the other hand, comes to the conclusion that between Dinu and Arjun there hardly exists any comparison. Her analysis provides a beautiful picture of these two men. This is a master stroke of characterisation, 'Arjun—you're not in charge of what you do, you're a toy, a manufactured thing, a weapon in someone else's hands. Your mind doesn't inhabit your body [...]. She saw that despite the largeness and authority of his presence, he was a man without resources, a man whose awareness of himself was very slight and very fragile; She saw that Dinu was much stronger and more resourceful [...]' (376). The inexplicable thing that we call depth and weight of personality is at the same time abstract and yet so real. At times it appears that it is the only thing that matters ultimately—an individual's ability of self-examination and introspection. Dinu is a person with this extraordinary quality of character. His involvement in his work of photography is complete. Once Alison wants to accompany him to his outdoor sites but Dinu is cold in his response. He actually loses himself completely in his work. Dinu and Alison are soon parted forever because of the war. The relationship that might have bloomed and lasted a lifetime is ruptured by the tumult of war. Alison dies. By the end of the novel, Dinu reappears. He is old and mellow. Photography is his profession. He has been living a quiet married life with a well-known Burmese writer. But the readers of this novel remember Dinu of young age who is sharp-edged in his intellectual capacities as well as behaviour.

Apart from characters, at the level of pure ideas also, this novel is very rich. There are relevant ideas on the process of civilization, wars and their futility, the concept of boundaries, colonisation, journey, hybridity, rootlessness, childhood and the process of growing etc. Out of these I wish to concentrate on two topics. The concepts of journey, home, movement, new places and rootlessness are more or less related. We may have some discussion on this. The second point of discussion at the level of ideas is colonisation. Ghosh's concern about colonisation is too great to be ignored.

The novel begins in a web of journey, chance, uncertainty and orphanhood. These are related. The roadside food stall (dhaba) is a well-recognised symbol of journey. The roadside food stall is also a place of current news, cheap food, cheap sex and temporary connections. The opening scene sets the mood of the novel. It is a novel about many places, war and displacement, exile and rootlessness. It also depicts human helplessness in such a scenario. All that a human being can do is try to adjust, compromise, live and above everything else form relationships. This forming of new bonds, mixing of races and castes is something that does not stop. After all, this is human life. The Collector at one point of the novel is intrigued when he comes to know of the pregnancy of Supayalat's first daughter. He is disgusted. He is at a loss. His sense of class and decency is deeply violated, 'Was this love then: this coupling in the darkness, a princess of Burma and a Marathi coachman; this heedless mingling of sweat?' (152). This saga of human weaknesses gives birth to the concept of hybridity. No race is pure; nor is any caste pure. There is no pure royal blood or anything like that. Life is mixing—DNA combinations and permutations. Saya John is a fine example of this breed of hybridity. His clothes are Western. He speaks English, Hindustani and Burmese. His face looks like that of Chinese. Saya himself makes fun of his amalgamated identity, '[...] They (Indian soldiers) asked me this very question: how is it that you who look Chinese and carry a Christian name, can speak our language? When I told them how this had come about, they would laugh and say, you are a *Dhobi Ka Kutta*—a washerman's dog—*Na Ghar Ka Na Ghat Ka*—you don't belong anywhere, either by the water or on land, and I'd say, yes that is exactly what I am.' He laughed, with an infectious hilarity and Raj Kumar joined in' (10). This is a laughter of mutual sharing. Raj Kumar is as much a washerman's dog as Saya John. There is no humiliation between the two. This is simple acceptance of fact.

Change, make-shift arrangements and temporary homes appear again and again in this novel. These things give this novel its contemporary flavour. By this sense of shifting only the novel comes close to the reader of the present times where movement and uncertainty have become the order of the day.

The process of colonisation and the state of the colonised are very relevant thought components of this novel. The very word used for Raj Kumar—Kaala—is objectionable to our generation, which is decolonised at least in the political sense of the word. What we witness in this text is the actual process of aggression, capture and colonisation. How the Burmese people are robbed of all grace with guns and artillery. The British are only giving commands. The soldiers who are invading Burma are Indians. Instead of fighting their common enemy— the British—the Burmese and the Indians are fighting among themselves. The scene of ousting of the deposed Burmese king is ironically tragic, 'In victory the British had decided to be generous [...] the British Government wished to provide them with an escort of attendants and advisors [...]. But now it was time to leave, the guard of honour was waiting (40-43). Guard of honour for a captive, dethroned king! Ghosh even mentions Bahadur Shah Zafar, the last Indian Emperor who was taken to

Rangoon in exile. A parallel is drawn here. One thing, apart from the cruel colonisation, must be said that these emperors were distanced from reality, from their own subjects and land to a shocking extent. When King Thebaw is taken out of his palace, it is for the first time he is seeing his land. Ghosh goes on ruthlessly describing the conditions of Indians in Burma who were taken there to work in the docks and mills, to pull rickshaws and empty the latrines' (49). Another shock comes when we learn that those who wait on Queen Supayalat are supposed to do so on all their fours *i.e.*, both hands and legs on floor. When an English midwife comes, she refuses to crawl. Supayalat fails to make her crawl; 'She was an English woman' (55).

Apart from these human scenes of colonisation, Ghosh also deals with the larger question of Europe's greed. Everything becomes a resource to be exploited—woods, water, mines, people, just everyone and everything. '[...] Resources were being exploited with an energy and efficiency hitherto undreamed of' (66). Forests are cut on a very mass scale without giving any thought to the hazards of environment that such an unthinking act would cause. Burma becomes the mine of wealth for the British. 'In a few decades the wealth will be gone—all the gems, the timber and the oil—and then they too will leave' (88).

Mental colonisation is even worse. For example, Saya does not see the English as usurpers. For him, they are superior. From them, he has learnt the art of using everything for his own benefit. The Europeans for him stand for efficient exploitation. To him, it brings profit. He does not know anything beyond his immediate gain, nor does he want to know. Many decades later we see Arjun boasting of his connection with Westerners. In his mind, he has accepted that the Western style is better and therefore desirable. 'Dinu understood that it was through their association with Europeans that Arjun and his fellow-officers saw themselves as pioneers' (279). We also see

Raj Kumar being convinced that without the British the Burmese economy would collapse (306). Many stances can be given where the author has shown the cruelty of colonisation and its impact on the lives and mind of the colonised. Decolonisation is not easy, perhaps it is not even possible. As Arjun says, 'We rebelled against an Empire that has shaped everything in our lives; coloured everything in the world as we know it. It is a huge, indelible stain, which has tainted all of us. We cannot destroy it without destroying ourselves' (518).

We can easily see as to why Ghosh withdrew *The Glass Palace* from Commonwealth Prize Short Listing. Commonwealth is a remnant of colonisation. The spirit of this book is anticolonial.

REFERENCE

Ghosh, Amitav. 2000. *The Glass Palace*. New Delhi: Ravi Dayal Publishers and Permanent Black.

Index